Four Questions About Violence

Insights from a
Forensic Psychiatrist

Dr Gwen Adshead

faber

First published in 2025
by Faber & Faber Limited
The Bindery, 51 Hatton Garden
London EC1N 8HN

Typeset by Faber & Faber
Printed and bound by CPI Group (UK) Ltd, Croydon, CR0 4YY

All rights reserved
© Gwen Adshead, 2025

The right of Gwen Adshead to be identified as author of this
work has been asserted in accordance with Section 77 of
the Copyright, Designs and Patents Act 1988

A CIP record for this book
is available from the British Library

ISBN 978–0–571–39509–5

Printed and bound in the UK on FSC® certified paper in line with our continuing
commitment to ethical business practices, sustainability and the environment.
For further information see faber.co.uk/environmental-policy

Our authorised representative in the EU for product safety is
Easy Access System Europe, Mustamäe tee 50, 10621 Tallinn, Estonia
gpsr.requests@easproject.com

2 4 6 8 10 9 7 5 3 1

To all those who survive human violence
and those who work with them
as they seek to transform their suffering

Contents

Author's note	1
1. Is violence normal?	7
2. Aren't they all evil?	23
3. Does trauma cause violence?	39
4. Can we change violent minds?	59
Afterword: Is there a link between human goodness and mental health?	75
Acknowledgements	93
Endnotes	95

Author's note

In May 2024 I got an email from the controller of Radio 4 inviting me to have lunch with him. To say I was startled by this invitation would be an understatement and, as I replied, I was aware of feeling irrationally anxious and even guilty, as if I was being summoned to the headmaster's office for an offence and should expect to be told off. What I did *not* expect was to be asked if I would be interested in giving the Reith Lectures later that year on the theme of violence. The controller explained that he felt that this theme was ripe for a public conversation, and I could only agree.

As the details of the Reith process were explained, I was grateful for my long experience in keeping my face neutral while hearing something you weren't expecting to hear. I found myself reminded of a therapy session with a patient in Broadmoor, who was recounting his difficulties in disposing of what he thought was a dead body. I remember nodding away as he detailed the struggle of trying to roll it up in a carpet and drag it out of the room, as if I too was entirely au fait with such problems.

I intend no disrespect to the controller of Radio 4 when I say that as he spoke, that macabre conversation came to mind. I might have appeared to be politely agreeing to the logistics of giving the Reith Lectures, but inside I was facing a new and unanticipated challenge: namely, how to roll up all I've learned about human violence in nearly forty years as a forensic psychiatrist and psychotherapist, and then both summarise it and make it come alive in four brief lectures for smart and serious people.

However, my memory of that Broadmoor conversation (and some others like it) prompted a possible way forward. In general, when facing an unusual and daunting task, it's often a good idea to divide it into manageable parts. One way presented itself to me, which was to consider the questions that have most often been put to me about work as a forensic psychiatrist and psychotherapist. One of the good things about forensic psychiatry is that it deals with questions about which most ordinary people have a view. Is violence normal? Is it the same as evil? Is violence caused by trauma? And can we do anything about it anyway? These are the four questions I've had to study, and also the ones which I am most commonly asked about work in prisons and secure hospitals, so they seemed to be a sensible theme for my Reith Lectures.

The study of human violence is vast and deep, and one that different academic disciplines have examined from different perspectives. These Reith Lectures have focused on relational violence, as opposed to the military and political sort, or that which arises from businesses like the trade in illegal drugs.[1] My perspective centres on the contribution of the perpetrator's mind, based on my experience as a forensic psychiatrist and psychotherapist who assesses and treats violence perpetrators in the criminal justice system, particularly those who are thought to be mentally unwell. These lectures therefore deal only with criminal violence in ordinary communities in peacetime, although I am aware of the enormous scholarship on political, community and military violence in different historical and cultural contexts. I have learned from a range of criminological studies of violence perpetrators and prisoners, and especially studies of the language of violence, because most of what I know about human violence is based on listening to perpetrators talk about past cruelties and offences. I refer often to perpetration of child abuse and homicide, not because other forms of violence are not important but because most of my work (either as a therapist or court-appointed expert) has been with these kinds of perpetrators.

Each lecture was given in a different place, and I tried to link the place with the theme where possible. The first lecture was in London (which by tradition is at the BBC's Broadcasting House), so I wanted to start with something general. The BBC (like all other forms of public media) reports repeatedly on violence, which risks making it seem normal. It therefore seemed appropriate to explore the question of the normality of violence at the home of the Reith Lectures.

The second lecture on the subject of evil and violence was at the new V&A building in Dundee, and was appropriate to present there because so much important and successful work on violence reduction has been done in Scotland. The third lecture on trauma was held at HMP Grendon, the oldest prison therapeutic community (PTC) in the UK. PTCs offer therapy to prisoners to help them understand their violence better, and there is good evidence that they play an effective role in offender rehabilitation. I am part of a group that provides some oversight and support for the work that Grendon does, and I have learned what good it does, so I am deeply grateful to the governor of Grendon and the Ministry of Justice for giving the Reith team permission to record the third lecture there.

The last lecture was in Norway, in the city of Bergen, because of the differing approaches to offender rehabilitation in the UK and Norway. The national policy of the Norwegian correctional system states that those sent to prison are punished *only* by their loss of liberty. This means that the primary task of the Norwegian prison system is not to humiliate or belittle prisoners, but to help them reduce their risk of reoffending on release. This policy is in stark contrast to what we offer in the UK, and so Norway was a fitting place for me to explore ways to help offenders change their minds for the better.

This book contains the essential texts of the four lectures as broadcast. However, the timings for radio inevitably constrained the length of the text, and this book has allowed me to expand on some issues. I have also included an additional essay addressing a question that I have often asked myself: namely, whether there is any link between being mentally well and acting well towards others.

Each lecture comes with some endnotes containing references that inform my thinking. However, I must offer the important caveat that the lectures do not offer any kind of systematic review of the literature on the different issues raised in them (which include not only criminal violence, but epigenetics, moral philosophy, attachment theory and gender roles). The endnotes are not in any way definitive and can only hint at the depth and breadth of the domains of study that are relevant to human violence.

A vital part of the Reith Lectures is the participation of the audience. We had different audiences in each location, and I am extremely grateful to all those who attended the lectures in person, and to those who asked such interesting questions. I am also grateful to all the people who took the time after the broadcasts to contact me with their feedback and responses, most of which were positive and sometimes thought-provoking. They were a potent reminder to me that violence is a subject that everyone has an interest in understanding, and that with courage and hope we can try to reduce it.

1: Is violence normal?

It is usual these days for lecturers about violence to offer a content warning. I shall use a quote by one of our earliest psychologists (possibly better known as a playwright):

> So shall you hear
> Of carnal, bloody, and unnatural acts,
> Of accidental judgments, casual slaughters;
> Of deaths put on by cunning and forc'd cause.
> *Hamlet*, Act V, Scene ii

This quote from Shakespeare's *Hamlet* articulates the first question. Is human violence natural or unnatural? We are social animals who resemble other primates in terms of making and maintaining relationships, and research with chimpanzees and baboons (who like ourselves live in groups) reports that these animals use violence against each other. Given that we share 98 per cent of our DNA with these group animals, it might seem safe to assume that violence is 'in our nature'. But the fact that something is natural does not mean it is normal: even chimpanzees have 'rules' about when they use violence in their social relationships, within their groups and without. For example, male chimps who are lower in the hierarchy are not 'allowed' to attack chimps who are higher-ranked, and those who do so are often 'punished' severely by attacks from others. Similarly, in baboon troops, a dominant group leader who is beaten by a younger, stronger rival is 'allowed' to be attacked by others, and some animals may choose to leave their troop and join another rather than be relentlessly beaten up by their own troop (ex-Tory party leaders take note).[1] And we should note how a 2 per cent difference in genetic make-up adds up to huge and significant differences in actions and relationships. As my dear father used to say, there are some similarities between a grizzly bear and a teddy bear, but the differences are much, *much* more important.

I wonder if we tend to normalise violence because we know somewhere, deep down, that we all have a capacity for cruelty. Any of us can experience, even briefly, the wish to hurt others who have enraged or frightened us. I'm sure you don't need any convincing – the fact that narratives of murder and cruelty have fascinated us for thousands of years and continue to do so is evidence of our awareness of this capacity. Greek tragedies, true crime, the enduring appeal of crime fiction: these are narratives that have puzzled and intrigued us for centuries. I am reminded now of a conversation in a therapy group for homicide perpetrators, in which one of the group members observed, 'Every night on the TV, you can watch a story of murder.'

Forensic psychiatrists are asked by courts to explore unusual acts of extreme violence and cruelty that seem to have no meaning or rational purpose to them, and give an opinion as to whether mental illness could explain that violence. What I have learned is that it is illuminating to listen to what perpetrators say about such unusual actions. The details of the bloody act are less interesting to me than its meaning and effects – for victim, perpetrator and those around them. I see my role as that of the naturalist observing the unusual and the unknown, keeping my eyes, ears and, above all, my mind open.

I hope it is obvious that attempting to understand violence in this way is not the same as excusing violence. Rather, it is my firm belief that listening to what perpetrators say about what they have done may offer insights into potential interventions for violence reduction and prevention. It is because violence can be bloody and dreadful that we must take it seriously and be willing to go deeper into the darkness of it, to try and understand what is being communicated.

Violence is unusual but not alien

One consequence of this fascination with violence is that we risk making assumptions about it: that it is all the same kind of behaviour, and that it is committed by 'monsters' with strange and alien purposes who are wholly other than us, with minds that are preoccupied only and always with violence.

Let's return to my patient in Broadmoor telling me about his experience of having to dispose of what he thought was a dead body. He faced a common problem for those who have committed a crime – how to get rid of the evidence. There is, naturally, no manual for this, and at that time, there was no internet to consult. My patient discovered that a human body is too heavy to move alone, and he told me how he felt forced to consider decapitation in order to make his task easier. He then considered how messy it might be, which might cause further problems (you can see now the absurdity of my nodding along as he talked).

My point here is this man did not relish his task, nor did he have a dark and obscure motive for contemplating dismemberment. He had a practical problem to solve, which reminded me of a reported interview with Dennis Nilsen (who killed several people and consigned their body parts to the drains).[2] Mr Nilsen commented that he was taken aback to find that the public seemed more shocked by what he had done to the bodies than the fact that he had killed in the first place. He was the son of a butcher, and dismemberment of the body was the horrible but practical solution to a major problem. And I am also reminded of a man who had done something similar, but found it hard to recall in therapy, saying to me, 'I can't imagine being the kind of person who would do such a thing.' Few of us can.

He's not an ordinary killer

Which takes me to my next point: that there is no such thing as a 'typical killer'. Human violence takes different forms: gang violence is different to domestic violence, and neither of these automatically lead to homicide. Homicide is different in different contexts, in its meaning and in its prevalence. It has a finality to it that changes the universe; as the Talmud* puts it, whoever takes one life takes the world entire. In the UK, we are lucky to live in a country whose homicide rate is way below the global average, so that homicide is a statistically rare event. In the year ending March 2023, there were 534 homicides in England and Wales, and 52 in Scotland: the lowest numbers for some time and consistent with the general decline in violence over the last thirty years.[3]

But of course, the rarity of some events is no indicator of how important they are, and each of those numbers represents a shattering catastrophe for a family. The apparently good news about falling homicide rates is no comfort to those bereaved by murder. When I wrote the first draft of this lecture in the summer of 2024, I was only too aware that the number of homicides would increase by the time my lectures went to air, as I listened to the reports of three children killed in Southport. Now, as I

---

* The primary source of Jewish religious law and theology.

update these lectures for publication, I fear that several more violent deaths have been added to the number for this year. I am reminded too of the piece by Fordyce Maxwell, written at the time of the Dunblane massacre, in which he said that homicide forces survivors to live in two worlds: a world of apparently ordinary function and an inner world of pain and chaos.[4]

The same torment can also be true of those people bereaved by homicide who were also the perpetrators of that homicide: people who had killed parents, siblings, children while mentally ill. Their illness made them 'see' their loved ones in a distorted light, and when their vision clears, they may be overwhelmed by grief and shock. Some even develop post-traumatic stress disorder (PTSD) in response to their own violence. I learned from colleagues at a forensic service in Connecticut who had set up a therapy group for these people, which had been of benefit to them and their surviving families. My psychologist colleagues and I decided to do something similar at Broadmoor Hospital for patients who killed when mentally ill. I am glad to say that our homicide groups (we needed more than one) have continued to meet weekly for twenty years, although the membership has changed, as have the staff who run them. But what we have learned so far from running these groups is that each perpetrator's story is different, and that the factors that lead to a killing are multiple and complex.

I'm reminded of another case I was consulted on, involving a man who had killed in highly unusual circumstances. His loyal and loving wife was quoted as pleading for understanding, saying, 'He's not an ordinary killer.' But I am now doubtful that there is such a thing as an 'ordinary killing'. It is true that until the 1990s, the Home Office used to somewhat oversimplify homicides by categorising them as either 'normal' or 'abnormal' in terms of motive. 'Normal' referred to those killings where the motive seemed to make some kind of human sense: those familiar human emotions like greed for money, rejection and jealousy, the wish for revenge or a substance-fuelled quarrel. The 'abnormal' homicides were those where the motive was obscure to those investigating or judging, and did not include killing that was found to be associated with mental illness. In only a few cases will mental illness seem to explain the killing, although this is unusual: people with severe mental illness account for only 5.3 per cent of recorded violence.[5]

It's also important to note that being found mentally ill at the time of a homicide does not automatically mean you will be found to be less responsible, and even if you are thought to be less responsible, you may still be sent to prison. Interestingly, it is not always the homicide perpetrators who struggle most with mental disorder and distress; it is often the *non-violent majority* of prisoners, typically young men and women with addiction and family breakdown issues, with previous histories of suicidal ideation, who struggle most with the kind of psychological pain and distress that puts people at high risk of suicide.[6]

The rarity of homicide doesn't minimise its importance but, rather, should make us more curious about it, not less. Even the apparently 'rational' or normal motives only make sense at the most superficial level: for example, if you want to make money, homicide is a high-risk, high-cost strategy which rarely works well. In the UK, like in similar social democracies in Europe, many homicides happen because of some kind of intense relational and personal disturbance. It is salutary to think that you are statistically most likely to kill or be killed by a person with whom you are or have been in an intimate relationship, especially if you are a woman.

But it's rare for these tragic events to happen at all, and perhaps that is why it is not unusual for people to assume that only an abnormal monster could inflict such dreadful damage on another person. But I no longer think this. Whenever I hear of some new and dreadful homicide, I think: Will we see that perpetrator in our hospital? Will he come to one of our therapy groups for people who've killed? Will she need help from the service for violent women in Bronzefield prison to which I offer support? What is there to know about what led up to the killing that may explain what they did and could help us try and reduce their future risk to others?

One thing we know is that strong emotions – both positive and negative – influence violence risk, especially in a relational context. Cast your mind back to the summer of 2024 and the weeks before the final of the Euros, when all sorts of emotions ran high: hope, suspense, anxiety, frustration. At such times, alcohol use soars, and apparently so can rates of domestic violence. A charity called Women's Aid cited research from an English study which found that men's violence to their wives and partners went up by 38 per cent if their team lost, as if abusers expel frustration and disappointment from their minds and onto the bodies of others. But the same study also found that men's violence increased by 26 per cent if their team *won*.[7] This data may just be a reminder that alcohol intoxication is one of the most potent risk factors for violence, but it also raises a question about the absence of the capacity for joy in the lives of men who hurt women, such that not even their team's success makes them feel better.

Unlocking violence; factors that lead to violence

What other risk factors for fatal violence do we need to think about? This question has been an important one for all those who are interested in homicide prevention, and especially for those professionals working with that rare group of people with severe mental illness who have been violent to others. The question 'Will he do it again?' becomes an urgent one and it cannot be simply answered. I am indebted to my colleague at Broadmoor, Peter Aylward, who first used the metaphor of a numeric-combination bicycle lock to describe how risk factors might come together to unlock violence. In this model, our capacity for violence is 'securely' contained most of the time, despite each of us having one or two risk factors which are not sufficient to unlock the violence.[8] It is only when enough risk factors are present that the last 'number' can click into place to complete the combination and unleash the violence.

Many of those factors are going to be *social* ones: lack of job opportunity, rigid beliefs about gender roles, and family conflict (as described by behavioural scientist Natalie Wilkins and colleagues for the Center for Disease Control in the USA[9]). Alcohol and substance misuse and addiction are ubiquitous and well-recognised factors for violence. But that final 'number' that 'unlocks' the violence is likely to be highly personal and meaningful for the individual perpetrator, and so can be different for each person. It could be as random as an offhand comment, a smile, an action perceived as a threat, a paranoid state of mind or even a football result. Whatever it is, what is unleashed is often a Hokusai wave of emotion that overwhelms the perpetrator and distorts how they see everything and everyone, especially the victim.

How we 'see' other people – in our mind's eye, as it were – can influence how we justify hurting them. There's an odd Pop Art picture (artist unknown) which has a magnified eye with a tear running out of it; the text reads 'We all think we're good people'. This is absolutely true to my experience; I don't think I have ever met anyone who said that they set out to be 'bad'. Rather, violence perpetrators usually have a story which both justifies and excuses their violence; what the criminologists first called in the 1950s a 'neutralisation discourse'.[10] A neutralisation discourse does what it says: it uses language to neutralise some kind of negative attribution or blame. One form of neutralisation is to blame the victim ('he started it'); another is to claim that the perpetrator only did what others do (normalising); while other forms include minimising the harm done to the victim and using their circumstances to excuse themselves ('I was drunk'). Sometimes a perpetrator will neutralise their actions by talking about their own victim experience ('you don't know what I've been through'). Using the metaphor above, we might say that perpetrators use language to identify their own bike-lock 'numbers' that explain what they have done. They normalise their own violence, try to make it understandable; they do not wish to be seen as 'monsters' but rather as people who felt they had no choice.

This claim to have had no choice at all is rarely true. Much of the work I do as a therapist is to help people come to see and accept that they did have choices, albeit limited and painful ones. This is a theme I will return to later; but at this point I am noting that violence perpetrators often struggle to make sense of what they have done, not seeing it as usual or normal for them. I have met the odd person who says flatly, 'I killed them; it's over, so what?' But even they will want to argue that they had their reasons, and that they are not monsters.

Violence as a communication

In our homicide groups, people usually begin by discussing what I think of as their 'cover story' about why they had killed, usually something that had been developed during their trial. Our group therapy process helps these men to revisit and dismantle that story, gradually going deeper into their accountability, and their guilt for what they had done. Eventually, each man describes how they came to kill, including the ways in which they convinced themselves that the killing was inevitable. By the time people leave the group, they usually understand how normalising killing as a solution made it more possible, that they are now responsible for keeping themselves mentally well, and that they must in future try to 'see' other people free of such distorted narratives.

I'm thinking now of Jack, who strangled his mother when he was mentally ill. He still seemed very unwell when he came to our Thursday group, and we guessed that being there was unsettling for him. But one day, after another member had been talking about his regrets about the past, he said abruptly, 'I wish I could say sorry to my mum for what I did . . . I know I was mentally ill, but I wish I could say how sorry I was and that she could forgive me. *I hope she understands how much I regret it.*' What was remarkable about this reflection was Jack's awareness of his sense of responsibility, although at trial he had been deemed not fully responsible because of his mental illness. Not only did he feel responsible, he was also seriously sad. We might also notice his use of the present tense in relation to his mother's mind, which suggests that he is not done grieving for her.

It was listening to men like Jack that made me realise that people who kill were not mindless monsters who'd been born to kill or who had murderousness running through their minds like a black thread in a complex carpet. More often, they seemed to be people like myself, who struggled with shame and guilt and other 'normal' human emotions. Yes, Jack had done something terrible which had changed his life, his identity and his family for ever. But he had not been a violent person all his life, and his fatal attack on his mother came out of the blue. He was an ordinary man who had done an extraordinary thing, and many homicide perpetrators are like this. That devoted wife I mentioned was trying to make this exact point; her husband was an ordinary, loving man, and his homicidal cruelty was not all he was. For both men, their violence was a dreadful and distorted communication from one human to another.

Violence: cruel, unusual and complex

I have made two arguments: first, that violence is not normal for humans, especially fatal violence; and second, that by normalising it, we risk failing to understand the complexity of the motives and circumstances that make a person see violence as a kind of solution. I passionately believe that if we want to reduce or prevent it, we need to understand all its causes and risk factors: what makes it start, what allows the risk to grow, and then, by allowing people to tell their stories, understand the final 'numbers' that can unlock that human capacity for cruelty and destructiveness. Denigrating, othering and calling perpetrators 'monsters' does nothing to decrease risk and may even make the problem worse, either because it gives perpetrators a kind of awful status that may excite some people to further violence or because it dehumanises perpetrators in ways that mirror what they did to their victims.

We ask our criminal courts to examine allegations of violence, determine guilt and also pass sentence on behalf of us all. The passing of that sentence represents our condemnation of violence, based on the social contract that when one of us is injured by it, we are all injured.

Comprehending and interpreting violence is part of our daily lives as citizens, and it is our duty to take that seriously. But I think we won't be able to do this if we oversimplify human violence and write off everyone who has killed or stalked someone, or abused a child, as mindless monsters, stuck in the malignant aspic of social media for ever, as if no one ever changed their mind for the better.

I think we all understand how 'monstering' people is one way to deal with rage and fear. These are human emotions that victims and perpetrators of violence share. We say that perpetrators need to manage those emotions, but we all have a responsibility not to get into those states of mind that might be called 'cruel and unusual'. What kinds of states these are is my next question.

2: Aren't they all evil?

'I have done evil things . . . but does that make me evil?' I have heard this question many times from the patients I work with as a forensic psychiatrist and psychotherapist. Typically, I begin my answer by telling them that evil is a complex idea, and that saints, sociologists, theologians and neuroscientists have all had something to say about it. But then I say to them that the capacity for evil is present in all of us; as William Blake said, 'Cruelty has a human heart.'[1]

I am going to suggest here, just as I do with my patients, that we must therefore attend to that capacity for cruelty in ourselves and study its components closely, because it is possible for each and every one of us to get into a state of mind that could be called 'evil'. I will also suggest that we need to manage our own capacity for evil by cultivating and practising our capacity for goodness, which is both protective against evil and healthy in its own right.

I've had to think about this issue in my work because, historically, there has been some confusion about mental illness and evil, and an implication that they are somehow connected. For example, hospitals like Broadmoor routinely used to be described as places that house 'evil' people. This false association extends even to the buildings, as we saw in the early summer of 2024, when some of the old nineteenth-century buildings that used to be Broadmoor Hospital caught on fire. The immediate reportage was all about the violent men who used to live there, most of whom are long dead. No mention of the firefighters or local householders who might have been at risk, or of the many men and women who successfully engaged in treatment in those buildings and who were enabled to either return to prison to pay their debt to society, or be rehabilitated safely in the community.

As I wrote in the previous lecture, what I am always struck by initially when I meet someone who has done a horrible thing is their ordinariness, and then, as they tell their story, the sense of a terrible intersection of chance and choices that led up to the killing, such that I usually feel that 'there but for the grace of God go I'. Often the only major difference between us is their long experience of severe mental illness, which sometimes results in people feeling possessed or compelled by an inner network of disorganised, even chaotic thoughts and feelings. Such emotions and thoughts are nearly always aggravated by alcohol and drug intoxication, and also intense levels of fear and distress, which distort people's sense of reality.

I guess we could think of the men and women I've seen in my work as people who were driven into evil states of mind by a fatal combination of mental illness, addiction and different kinds of stress. Whatever the combination of risk factors, the violence committed by the people in our secure hospitals and prisons seems far from ordinary, especially when we consider that the vast majority of people with mental illness, even severe mental illness, pose no risk of harm to anyone else.[2] I sometimes think of the people I work with as the human version of a natural disaster; as one of my patients said recently, 'I was like a tornado in the path of my victim.'

Evil as ordinary

Poetry, drama and history tell us that ordinary men and women can get into evil states of mind. The poet W. H. Auden describes evil as 'unspectacular and always human',[3] and the historian Christopher Browning called his study of members of a German reserve police battalion who killed thousands of innocent civilians *Ordinary Men*.[4] Browning's work is a must-read for anyone who is interested in the evil state of mind, and one of his most interesting findings is that not all these men (many of whom had served as soldiers in World War I) felt the same about their murderous orders. Only about a third of them seemed to relish their task, about a third saw themselves as under quasi-military obedience, leaving about a third who resisted by seeking a transfer away from this detail. It has been suggested that the emotional impact of this type of killing on military morale was reported to the Nazi high command and was one factor that led to the development of the technology of mass murder and the death camps.

The sentencing statistics for homicides show that only a minority of people are found to be mentally unwell at the time of the killing and that most perpetrators are seen as ordinary people who killed for an ordinarily unpleasant reason. That does not mean that ordinary homicide perpetrators are all unfeeling and cold; many experience painful and disturbing emotions, and the killing provides some sense of release. But then afterwards, the same people who have killed also suffer remorse and distress, especially those who kill family members, and they are known to be at increased risk of suicide. Parents who kill their children are at especially high risk of suicide later, a risk that persists for years. I shall never forget the young mother who killed her children while suffering a postnatal mental illness. She was sent to hospital for treatment, but recovery brought intolerable insight and distress. We knew she was at high risk of suicide even as we planned for her return to the community, and sure enough, she took her own life on her release, some ten years after her offence.

I am also thinking of all those young men who are killed by other young men. For the year ending March 2023, 71 per cent of homicide victims in England and Wales were male, and the same percentage was seen in Scotland. But in England and Wales, it is the *youngest* men whose risk of being a victim is higher than the national average, especially those aged sixteen to twenty-four.[5] They kill and they die in an aroused and intoxicated state of mind that goes looking for a fight, that is both dreadful and ordinary. It is a state of mind that is generally quite *unlike* the state of mind we tend to call 'evil', because it is impulsive, driven by 'hot' emotions like anger, and the suffering caused is unplanned and disorganised. It actually has more in common with states of mind that arise in severe mental illness, where reality is greatly distorted, which is why the combination of mental illness and substance misuse significantly increases risk.

Elements of the evil state of mind

So, what are the factors that make up the evil state of mind? I think there are seven psychological elements which are distinct but related to each other. It is rare for these factors to be present all at once, but a certain number of them are probably essential for more extreme cruelty to take place. The first factor is what is called 'cognitive distortion', i.e. disturbance of the ordinary capacity for flexible and nuanced thinking, especially in a social context, both small and large scale. A key aspect of cognitive distortion is *rigidity* of thinking about others and the person's absolute certainty regarding their beliefs about the world. I am thinking here about those men who are certain that they can tell what a woman is thinking, or those who have no doubt at all that the world is divided into winners and losers. In such a state of mind, there is no capacity to tolerate uncertainty or ambiguity, to say, 'I don't know what's going on here.'

Such distortions are further aggravated by how information is weighed, and the discounting of any information that contradicts one's thinking. This psychological rigidity and exclusion of uncertainty contributes to the development of the second factor of evil states of mind, which is hyper-individualism and egocentricity. This is a mental perspective in which other people's minds are neither real nor morally significant.

Such rigid certainty and egocentricity then fuel the third factor, which is the feeling of entitlement to control and wield power over others, which is absolute. I read recently about the trial of a man in his early twenties who attacked a much older woman he met on his way home from the pub. She pleaded with him to leave her alone, and he replied, 'I'm the boss now, you have to do what I say.' He apparently sobbed in the dock as he was sentenced for rape and GBH; he was previously an ordinary young man with a long-term girlfriend who was expecting their child (whom he would probably never know). He is an example of how an evil state of mind need not be enduring, nor be a persistent personal characteristic, and may even co-exist with a capacity for goodness towards others. We have no details about his insight or what he felt about his victim, but my point here is only that he was ordinary in terms of having a capacity for making relationships and working. Such a history makes him quite *unlike* the men who get admitted to places like Broadmoor, who rarely have enduring relationships with anyone.

The fourth component of the evil state of mind is the setting-up of one's own personal moral rule book and an assumption of a godlike omnipotence, which again ignores social traditions and denigrates the idea of the common good. Primo Levi, a writer who was a prisoner in Auschwitz, tells a story of a time when he witnessed a guard brutally hitting a prisoner for no reason. The prisoner protested, 'Why did you do that?', seeking a rational, social understanding of what had happened (not least so he could avoid it again in future). But the guard replied, 'There is no "why" here,' communicating that both he and the prisoner were now in a world with a completely different and idiosyncratic moral framework and values.

Levi's example is naturally connected with the fifth component of the evil state of mind, namely conscious denigration of victims, their vulnerability and their suffering. This denigration is the essence of the cruelty that we fear most about evil, and rightly so. Evil states of mind need a target, someone to denigrate and despoil and whose suffering proves to the perpetrator that they are all-powerful and cannot be gainsaid. In this state of mind, the perpetrator sees the victim's vulnerability as evidence that the victim is disgusting or dishonourable, which justifies their cruelty and may even enhance their status. Justified cruelty is often legitimised by pre-existing narratives about victims, both rigidly held and regularly elaborated. The development of such narratives happens at the level of the personal and the social, especially long-held and re-rehearsed stories of past humiliation and dishonour which must be avenged. National and international experts on violence have commented on the danger to societies when such revenge narratives are woven into gender-role expectations of what it is to be a man.

The sixth component of the evil state of mind also involves the creation of narratives which dehumanise victims. But this process is not as simple or binary as it sounds. It used to be thought that dehumanising people was essential to cruelty because it allowed the perpetrator some moral numbing or distance from being judged negatively. But it is clear from studies of everyday atrocities that people in an evil state of mind may seek to preserve the humanity of victims in their minds as part of the infliction of suffering. I am thinking here of the man who killed his child in front of his wife to punish her for leaving him. In that moment, he needed her to be human in order that she fully experience the suffering he planned for her.

Self-deception and blindness

The final component of the evil state of mind involves self-deception and rejection of the idea that there is something called 'truth' which (as the seventeenth-century philosopher John Locke put it) is worth the seeking. All the components of the evil state of mind are interconnected, but arguably this last component enables and concentrates all the others. Disinformation and self-deception are old problems for human relationships, and they can be present at the social-community level, as well as the individual.

Let me offer two different examples, both of which I know only by report. Many years ago, a businessman was jailed for fraud, which is, on the face of it, a non-violent crime and perhaps not obviously evidence of an evil state of mind. His crime was to make and sell items which he claimed were landmine detectors, although he knew they were nothing of the sort.[6] He must have known that people would go looking for landmines, trusting in the useless device for which he had charged them a lot of money. It is not known how many people died because of his idea of a successful business, and he seems not to have cared to know.

My second example is more recent and is based on the reporting of riots in the summer of 2024. Social unrest and rioting broke out in different parts of the country after reports of the murders of children in Southport.

Some individuals spread disinformation about the identity of possible suspects on social media and incited violence against them. Again, on the face of it, these are non-violent offences which might not fit with commonplace notions of evil, and I suspect that those who posted false information have almost nothing in common with the people I see in prisons or secure psychiatric care. Yet accusing a person of heinous acts without any evidence – or even while knowing that it is not the case – is an act of cruelty, if only because it shows an absence of concern about what might happen as a result of that accusation.

The incitements to violence against vulnerable others also suggest an explicit view that it is okay to hurt, and to wish to hurt, people you have decided to dislike, *even if you have never met them*. We cannot know for sure, but I suspect those who posted disinformation told themselves that they were good people doing a good thing, and either blinded themselves to the consequences or felt entitled to harm others whom they did not like (which is grandiosity), and so did not care. It is noteworthy that more than one of those who posted such false and cruel disinformation had no history of criminality or any kind of antisocial behaviour. On the face of it, they were ordinary members of the public, and they included women with children.

People who don't care: psychopathy

In these people's actions, we see some evidence of the elements that make up an evil state of mind. Such people, who lack care or concern for others they don't know, probably pose no immediate danger to citizens they *do* know, but could that change? Would you like such a person to care for your children or be your doctor? This was a question raised in the 1940s by a psychiatrist called Hervey Cleckley, who came across patients in his hospital who did not seem to care about the distress they caused others, and were similarly grandiose when challenged. Cleckley said this state of mind was an example of 'psychopathy', and he called it a kind of 'agnosia' or inability to 'see' others as people. He was puzzled by the fact that many of his 'psychopaths' had what he called 'a mask of sanity': they appeared generally to be ordinary, even privileged folk, who nonetheless continued to lie, con and exploit others.

It is important to note that Cleckley's work did not identify psychopaths as either 'evil' or violent necessarily. But his findings were later used by Professor Robert Hare in 1990 to create a checklist of aspects of psychopathy, which he applied to men serving time in prison for violent offences.[7] Professor Hare wanted to improve risk assessment in violence perpetrators, and there is no doubt his work has been both valuable and influential for those who work with violence perpetrators and assess their risk. But

I think what is most noteworthy is that *not all* the violence perpetrators satisfied Professor Hare's criteria for psychopathy, which means that psychopathy doesn't explain all violence and is not a synonym for 'evil'.

So far, I've argued that (a) evil states of mind differ from the states of mind we see in those people with mental illness who are violent; and (b) that ordinary men and women can get into those states of mind. So, the question is, what can drive people into such states of mind? One approach, from the perspective of individual emotions, was first described in pre-classical thought, but is probably better known in its Christian elaboration as the seven deadly sins.

Each of the seven 'sins' actually reflects a kind of human emotion or self-related belief. Pride is traditionally seen as the deadliest sin, as an emotion which leads naturally to grandiosity and denigration of others. Both gluttony and lust describe dysregulated emotions as well as appetites. Greed and envy link directly to public discourses about whether there is enough to go round and the extremes of inequality that can be drivers of violence.[8] Sloth is probably better understood as a kind of ultimate in not-caring and a withdrawal from the world, and may be a driver for despair, which is a risk factor for suicide (and potentially for homicide also).

Anger is a complex emotion, not least because it can be both healthy (if properly managed) and also unhealthy. Anger is also a response to pain and threat: pets bite or hiss if they are in pain, and many theorists have argued that the anger that causes violence is a reaction to fear. But anger is also a potent risk factor for violence, because in its unhealthy, pathological form it can lead to hatred, which is an emotion that creates destructive bonds between potential perpetrators and their victims.

We all have to live with and learn to manage such emotions, which is partly the basis for my assertion that the capacity for evil is there to be found in all of us; it is, as St Thomas Aquinas suggested, a disposition in humans that may never be enacted but could be, in the right circumstances. But those circumstances may not always be down solely to our individual personalities and beliefs. We are social animals who are influenced by how others think and feel, and as we have seen, by the stories we hear and listen to. As described above, media of different sorts affect the way we think and feel about our place in society, our bonds to others and whom we may legitimately dislike or even despise. The reason that Nazi Germany is so often cited in the context of evil is that it is an example of what happens when the majority of a social community (including those with leadership roles) inhabit an evil state of mind which is legitimised at a national and cultural level. Such social structures and beliefs may resonate and amplify those aspects of the individual personality that can be activated to make evil states of mind seem both reasonable and satisfying.

Preventing the growth of evil

I want to return to my initial argument: that the evil state of mind is one that all of us can get into. Even the most ordinary person can bring themselves to carry out terrible cruelty while telling themselves that they are doing good. But we need to think about how evil starts and grows mentally, and where and how it seems likely to flourish, and where and how it can be discouraged. For example, spending time ruminating on greed, lust, anger, envy and pride, whether on your own or on social media, is the kind of activity which could edge you towards an evil state of mind. It might seem far away right now, but if other traumatic and stressful things happen to you (which they can even in the happiest of lives), you might find yourself developing a state of mind where cruelty to others doesn't seem so bad. We can then, in fact, begin to mirror the evil that we denigrate, fear and despise in others.

I like organic rather than mechanical metaphors for the human mind, so let me suggest that individual and social minds are like gardens that need close tending or else the boundaries will be lost and the weeds will choke the desired growth to death. I want to close by continuing this metaphor in relation to the importance of the cultivation of goodness in the individual mind and in communities. If evil is the relative absence of goodness (which I have seen in my practice), we need to 'grow' goodness using organic and dynamic qualities in our lives as humans. Practising compassionate and grateful states of mind can lead to the growth of virtues which act as a protection against evil states of mind. We have good reason to think that people, like plants, flourish in rich soil that is full of nutrients and water, and that forms part of a complex biosystem involving other plants, insects and birds. Neglect of the complexity of individual and social minds alike can lead to the social 'garden' being overtaken by ideologies that are like knotweed – damaging and hard to root out. I do not spend time in digital places like X precisely because it seems to me to be such an unhealthy place to be.

To grow a capacity for goodness paradoxically includes paying attention to our most painful and afflictive emotions, like anger, envy, vengefulness, grief and fear. If we are able to recognise such emotions within ourselves and then take the time to look at them and name them for what they are, we may be better able to consider them compassionately and carefully. When we do this, it gives us the mental space to think about these emotions and see them as events in the mind and not identities to inhabit. We then have more ways to manage painful emotions without harming ourselves or others; we can become what mindfulness practitioners call 'more skilful'.

So I am concluding that defending against evil states of mind means developing a capacity to take horrible emotions like rage and hatred seriously. We especially need to recognise in ourselves the kind of anger that leads to a wish to hurt others, so that we have more agency to protect ourselves. This may be essential right now, when social minds and movements around us appear to be drifting into a wilderness of cruelty and grandiosity. Experiencing the wish to hurt others is an especially important problem for those who have suffered trauma, and for whom managing anger may be a constant struggle. It is the connection between experiencing trauma and later violence that I discuss next.

3: Does trauma cause violence?

'Trauma' is a word that means many things in everyday speech, but my definition of trauma is that it is the kind of suffering that pierces your defences and gets under your psychological skin. I'm going to begin my exploration by asking you to cast your mind back to the year 1994, and to an American case where two brothers, Lyle, aged twenty-one, and Erik, nineteen, were tried for the murder of their parents, who had been shot at close range in their home in California. Their story may be familiar because (completely coincidentally) it has recently been the subject of both a crime-drama series and a documentary on Netflix.

The Menendez brothers did not deny that they killed their parents but claimed that they had done so because they were in fear of their lives after years of different kinds of abuse by their parents. Erik's allegation that he was sexually abused by his father was especially emphasised. The brothers claimed that they were suffering from PTSD as a result of the trauma they experienced, and their defence team instructed a psychiatrist, who gave expert testimony that supported their claim. If successful, the brothers could have been convicted of a lesser charge, such as manslaughter.

But in an adversarial system there is always an alternative account of what happened. The prosecution claimed that the brothers killed in order to get their inheritance. Their parents were wealthy people, and initially, the brothers told the police that their parents had been victims of a robbery. The prosecution also brought in their own psychiatrist, whose expert testimony vigorously rebutted the idea that having PTSD might not only explain the killing but mitigated criminal responsibility for it. Even if the brothers had PTSD, that could not 'prove' that they had been abused by their parents, and I suspect that he also pointed out that most victims of violence with PTSD are never violent to anyone. The jury found the prosecution evidence more convincing, and both brothers were found guilty of murder and sentenced to life without parole.

Intriguingly, the Netflix publicity prompted a review of the severity of the brothers' sentences, and they were given permission to apply for resentencing. The outcome was that they are now eligible for parole. But this change of mind towards the brothers is based on the assumption that what they said about their parents at the time of the trial was true, as if that allegation had not been examined in detail during the original trial. It is perhaps also worth noting that there are friends and relatives of the victims who objected strongly to this change of sentence, arguing that the victims had been labelled unjustly as 'child abusers' and could not defend themselves.

Can abuse excuse violence?

The Menendez trial was probably the first in which the phrase 'the abuse excuse' was used to advance the argument that the experience of being a victim of violence may be associated with becoming a perpetrator subsequently. I certainly recalled this case some years later, when I was working with a patient in therapy; let's call him Kevin. Many years before we met, when he was just nineteen, Kevin had killed and raped an elderly woman. He was deemed to be mentally unwell at the time of the offence and was sent to hospital for treatment. This included medication, and also having therapy to explore and, if possible, understand how he had come to do this dreadful thing.

Kevin and I met regularly for many months. We did not dwell on the grim details of what he had done, although we acknowledged them and referred to them as necessary. We did talk, however, about his abusive and traumatic childhood, and wondered together whether there was some link between the cruel intrusions perpetrated on his body and the similar intrusions he inflicted on the body of a complete stranger. I remember Kevin turning this idea over in his mind, and then saying, 'But I don't see how that would explain what I did. Most people who are abused as children don't go on to do what I did.'

Both the Menendez case and Kevin's question articulate the theme of this lecture. Could being a victim of violence in *some* circumstances make you more likely to become a perpetrator of violence? Was W. H. Auden right when he wrote, in 1939, 'Those to whom evil is done do evil in return'?[1] And, if so, how could the experience of intense levels of fear and distress make you more likely at some point to act violently towards others?

I think it's important to distinguish this theme of how experiencing trauma might increase violence risk from the idea of getting revenge. The philosopher Francis Bacon described revenge as a 'kind of wild justice',[2] and it is noteworthy that the Menendez brothers did not argue revenge at their trial. The state of being vengeful is seen as normal and cannot be an excuse for violence. Instead, the defence argued that the impact of repeated exposure to fear and distress in childhood had led to the development of mental disorders in adulthood, which could make a person pathologically sensitive to perceived threat and likely to overreact in an impulsive way.

Childhood adversity and health in adulthood

The question of how and whether childhood experience affects who you are as an adult is an old one, but it is only in the twentieth century that we have had the research tools to try and answer it. Ironically, around the same time as the Menendez trial, a large-scale study was being carried out in the USA to look at one particular aspect of this question: namely, whether exposure to childhood adversity and trauma can affect physical health in adulthood. The researchers devised a list of adverse childhood experiences (ACEs), such as growing up with quarrelling parents, parents with addiction or parents who had gone to prison, as well as more direct experiences of neglect and abuse (verbal, physical, sexual). It is important to note that you can be exposed to high levels of childhood trauma and adversity *without anyone laying a finger on you*.

The researchers then sent a questionnaire to people who used a general physical health care service and asked them to tick off on the list whether they had experienced *any kind* of childhood adversity. They then examined if there was a relationship between how much adversity they had suffered and their use of health care services. The results were published in 1998, and they were interesting.[3] Of the 13,000 people approached, nearly 10,000 replied. About 10 per cent of those who responded had experienced four or more kinds of childhood trauma, and they were much more likely to suffer poor physical health in the form of heart, respiratory and liver disease. This group were also more likely to be heavy smokers and drinkers and to be users of drugs, both prescribed and non-prescribed. In contrast, about 30 per cent of the people who responded had experienced no childhood adversity at all, and they had much better physical health. Similar research had been published in a UK study the previous year, and many comparable studies across the world have replicated the findings. These studies also find that high levels of exposure to childhood adversity are bad for your mental health, especially in increasing the risk of developing addiction and depression.[4]

All these studies suggest that if you receive a high 'dose' of trauma in childhood, this makes you vulnerable to developing a range of physical and mental health problems in adulthood. The implications are serious, especially in relation to public health. Both the World Health Organization (WHO) and the Center for Disease Control in the USA now encourage study of ACEs in order to improve public health. A recent WHO collaboration with Liverpool John Moores University and Public Health Wales (2023) published details of levels of ACEs in countries around the world.[5] In most European countries, only a minority of people have experienced *no* childhood adversity, and a smaller minority have experienced high levels of childhood trauma. There are differences between countries: for example, in Wales 14 per cent of the population have experienced four or more kinds of childhood trauma, but in England only 9 per cent and in Sweden just 1 per cent. In a related survey of young people aged sixteen to twenty-five from many different European countries, about 6 per cent reported very high levels of childhood trauma, most commonly the early death of a parent, physical abuse and family violence.

Downstream wreckage: the later risky effects of childhood trauma

There is general consensus that there is a link between exposure to high levels of childhood trauma (especially maltreatment by adults) and a range of problems in adulthood; not just poor mental and physical health, but also social problems, including criminal rule-breaking, interpersonal problems, substance misuse and addiction. But there is considerable debate about *how* exposure to childhood adversity could lead to problems in adulthood. How could repeated and persistent experiences of fear, pain, rage and terror cause so many problems in adulthood, the kind of problems that one study memorably describes as 'downstream wreckage'.[6]

There are a number of theories but no definitive answers, chiefly because good-quality research on these questions involves studying multiple factors in large groups of children over time, which is both expensive and tricky. Children's minds and brains develop and change at different rates at different ages in response to stressors within themselves, in their families and in their environments. Social stressors like poverty and/or discrimination and prejudice of any kind can also interact with individual trauma to affect development. Adolescence is an especially complex time to experience trauma, as a young person's brain development is influenced by (a) massive changes in hormone levels during puberty and (b) the equally massive psychosocial task of developing the basis of an adult identity outside the family. It is really no surprise that the majority of mental health problems begin in adolescence.

One theory is that a child who is exposed to high levels of stress, fear and rage will develop a chronic stress response that may be physically damaging to their developing brain. High levels of adrenaline and cortisol may impair the normal developmental trajectory of how brain connections form, especially connections between the frontal cortex and the limbic system (both of which are thought to be important in relation to emotional regulation and social decision-making).[7] It has also been argued that high levels of stress in early childhood may impair the normal development and function of the immune response in the child, leading to widespread inflammatory processes across the developing parasympathetic nervous system.

There has been particular interest in how exposure to trauma might distort the development of the vagus nerve, because of its unconscious influence on the activation of the muscles of the face, as well as heart and lung activity. Underactivity of the vagus can have an impact on the facial expressions people use in social situations, including social communications, and this is important because as group animals we need to be able to make connections when we feel anxious. However, the process of connection can also be a natural source of feeling anxious and uncertain.[8]

Epigenetics: how genes change in response to environments

Another theory involves epigenetics: the way that genetic expression can be affected by environmental factors, such as experiencing fear. Genes cannot affect human actions directly; rather, they affect the development of the brain by changing the nature of proteins that are necessary for cell growth and function in the brain. Any change in genetic expression can have an effect at the level of neuronal development. For example, we know that if pregnant women are exposed to high levels of stress (such as starvation or fleeing war-torn countries), they will respond with high levels of circulating stress hormones in their blood.[9] But their blood is then shared with their unborn babies through the umbilical cord, and high levels of maternal stress hormones can affect the genetic expression of those same hormones in the baby's brain (especially those relating to cardiovascular tone, insulin production and the hormones that help reduce stress reactions, called glucocorticoids). When born, these babies appear to have a lower threshold for stress sensitivity. It is relevant to note that in monkeys, a mother's social ranking status can also be a stressor that affects the epigenetic development of her baby's brain.

So far we have been talking about the impact of trauma on the child's brain and body. We now need to discuss the psychological impact of trauma on the developing *mind*, and especially a child's sense of themselves and their relationships with others. During the first five years of life, the child's mind changes from that of a hard-to-read infant, who has to learn how to communicate with their carers and make sense of their own bodies, to that of a small person, who has a definite sense of physical and mental self and a story to tell of who they are and who is important to them. Babies have to grow a *relational* mind that allows them to work out who they are as a person, who others are and, especially, who they want to get close to when they feel scared. Learning to manage painful emotions by getting close to someone and sharing your feelings in words is one of the most important tasks of early and late childhood, and it is facilitated if children can build secure attachments to adults they can trust and don't fear.

Attachment and trauma

The study of human attachment has been important for understanding both the ordinary development of social relationships between children and their carers, and what happens when that ordinary process is disrupted. As I emphasised in my first lecture, evolutionarily, we are similar to other primates who live in groups and who have to make relationships with others that persist across time – for protection, reproduction and just for companionship.

But that 2 per cent genetic difference between us and our nearest primate relative gives us a much bigger orbitofrontal cortex in terms of volume and number of brain connections (as well as some important differences in posture and head and neck development). These vital neocortical differences may account for why we have developed such an extensive capacity for language and symbolic representations of the world around us, and how we can make and maintain relationships with others in different groups successfully across a lifespan, while also embodying an individual sense of self.[10]

Arguably the reason that the first relationships with others that we form as babies and children are crucial is because they act as a template for later relationships. The evidence for this argument comes from studies of childhood attachments in humans and in other animals who, like us, grow up in groups and maintain bonds across a lifespan. We know about the importance of a positive attachment experience (which is termed 'secure') because we have a lot of data about what happens if you disrupt attachment security, in both animals and humans. If you disrupt attachments in group animals like monkeys by raising them in social isolation (which is highly stressful), this leads them to have an insecure attachment system, which then affects how they interact with other members of their monkey troop when they are reintroduced to the group as adults. These insecure monkeys find it hard to make relationships with other monkeys, and so are slow to mate and reproduce. The young, insecure males mounted high-risk attacks on older, higher-ranking monkeys, and the females were at risk of attacking their own offspring when they had them.[11]

The study of attachment in humans looked first at the ordinary development of attachments between mothers and children in different cultures and countries, and then expanded to look at what happens when children's attachments to their carers are compromised by different kinds of trauma: for example, gross emotional deprivation and neglect, active maltreatment (both emotional and physical), and ordinary but distressing family events that disrupt attachment, such as living with a parent who is chronically ill, frightened or distressed.

Mentalising and other minds

What has emerged from these studies is that secure attachment is essential for developing a 'social mind', i.e. a mind that can recognise others as real and embodied, just as you are. If you have a social mind, you can 'mentalise' your own mind and the minds of others: you know how you feel and think and can imagine how other minds that are different from yours can think and feel. 'Mentalising' is in effect the skill of how we 'see' and 'read' our own minds and the minds of others, and it is an aspect of our 'social mind' that is strongly associated with attachment security.

Poor mentalising is common; in fact, we all struggle with mentalising at times, and especially if we are stressed or unwell. But what studies of insecure attachment in children have found is that attachment insecurity can lead to the inability to make trusting relationships with others, and it is this that seems to impair the development of mentalising skills. Without an ability to trust, the child does not know how to seek help from others when vulnerable, and they may develop a habit of deactivating their minds when vulnerable so that they do not feel anxious. But if you cannot learn to feel and think about your own anxiety by yourself and with others, your capacity to see your own mind as real is impaired, and other people may not seem very real to you either.[12] For example, an early study looked at how young children reacted to their image in a mirror, and found that abused children were more likely to react to their image with hostility and fear, compared to those who had not been abused. They were also children who lacked language for painful emotions. Children who are maltreated are more likely to have cognitive deficits, problems with self-recognition and self-esteem, and problems with reality-testing and how they appraise social situations.[13]

These are good examples of impairments in mentalising that could lead to problems later, and especially problems in relating to others. There have been several studies that have suggested that the failure to 'consider' or 'read' other people's intentions skilfully may be one factor that makes people more prone to use violence. I am thinking now of a sad case in which a young man attacked an older man in the street. The older man had reprimanded him for something minor, and the young man (a teenager, really) flew into a rage and beat the man to death. As his victim lay dying, the perpetrator was heard to shout, 'What you saying now? What you saying now?', as if he was carrying on some kind of argument in his head with his victim.

Something in the victim's voice and language activated feelings of shame and rage, which this young man could not manage or make sense of. He could only embody that emotion and then evacuate it into another body, with fatal and tragic results. Things might have been different if he had learned how to mentalise and articulate painful emotions, and to bear them without action, a capacity that we generally learn from being cared for and cherished.

There are other examples of how mentalising failures can increase the risk of violence. A lowered threshold for threat perception could increase the risk of responding to threat that is not actually there. There is evidence that some violence perpetrators are prone to misreading threat in other people's faces and react to socially ambiguous situations as if they were threats. Children who are exposed to multiple kinds of trauma may grow up to become teenagers who dislike themselves and fear others. These are the teenagers and young adults who struggle to articulate painful emotions like shame, sadness and hate, instead drowning them in alcohol or numbing them with drugs. It is this group who may become the small proportion of teenage offenders who commit violence persistently, from late childhood into adulthood. This group may also turn to self-harm and have increased risk of suicide; the 2023 study on ACEs by WHO and Public Health Wales reported that exposure to high levels of ACEs substantially increases suicide risk.

That report also stated *unequivocally* that exposure to childhood trauma increases the risk for being both a victim and a perpetrator of violence, and that the two states might be connected. A population study of teenagers in Finland also found strong evidence that suffering traumatic stress in childhood leads to a threefold increase in the risk of committing violence in *both* sexes, although the effect is stronger for boys. Parental education was a noteworthy protective factor: families where parents had less education were more likely to be families where there was trauma. A different kind of population study in the USA also found that both boys and girls who had experienced multiple kinds of victimisation were at increased risk of violent actions when they got older, including intentional physical harm, causing injury that needed medical attention, and intimate partner violence.[14] Yet another study published in 2024 found that in one US state, people with high levels of childhood adversity were nearly twice as likely as people with low levels of childhood adversity to keep a gun in the house.[15]

But there are caveats to these studies that are important to consider. They often involve meta-analyses of smaller studies, which may be subject to publication bias that favours studies that do show an association between ACEs and violence, and not those which don't. Although the data look promising, they do not definitively show that adverse childhood experiences *inevitably* cause violence. Nor does exposure to childhood trauma *predict* violence risk: it is still the case that not everyone who is maltreated and abused as a child goes on to be delinquent or a perpetrator; the cycle of violence is not a perfect circle.[16] Of all teenagers who get into trouble in their teens, it is a small subgroup only who go on to be chronic, severe violent offenders, and the proportion of risk due to childhood trauma may interact with other risks that might arise from living in social environments which are subject to stressors like high unemployment, community violence, lack of social support and poor literacy.[17]

It is a minority of socially and psychologically disadvantaged people who are at increased risk of criminal rule-breaking generally, which in turn increases the risk of criminal violence. Most people with poor mentalising skills, low self-esteem and mental illness will never be violent to anyone except themselves. And although substance misuse, addiction and antisocial attitudes are known risk factors for violence, most antisocial addicts will not become violent. As my patient understood all those years before, childhood trauma is not a complete explanation for violence. Nor can trauma excuse violence, and the question of whether it can mitigate culpability is a question for juries and courts, not academic study.

Some final thoughts: the role of gender

In exploring the question of whether trauma causes violence, I have to conclude that there is compelling evidence that childhood trauma is one risk variable for violence in some groups of people. But questions remain about who is especially vulnerable, and what protective factors might be operating in those who do not go on to be violent. We might be especially interested in how promoting society cohesion as a sense of community acts as a protective factor for some young people, especially in the years of emerging adulthood and access to work and employment opportunities.

There are so many questions to consider. I want to close by raising two that I find especially puzzling. First, why do males outnumber females by nine to one as violence perpetrators? Large-scale studies suggest that boys and girls experience similar levels of abuse, and many people have argued that young women and girls experience more abuse and suffer more because of it. But only a fraction of abused boys and girls will go on to be violent, and only a highly unusual minority of women will be violence perpetrators. It seems that although women are often traumatised in childhood and adulthood, they are able (in the main) to protect themselves from becoming perpetrators (even allowing for those women who use verbal and emotional violence, and those who make alliances with violent men to commit violence).

So there is a question in my mind about the gender-role stereotypes and associated role expectations. Could there be a connection with the experience of abuse and toxic gender-role expectations for *both* men *and* women? One risky gender-role stereotype (beloved by all kinds of media) is that women are always vulnerable, but men are 'never' seen as such, instead only as predators. But we know that significant subgroups of boys and girls will be vulnerable to different kinds of trauma, which means that we run the risk of distorting reality by not letting men sometimes be seen as vulnerable, and women sometimes as strong. If we deny and denigrate male vulnerability, could this make boys more likely to develop toxic internal narratives of both masculinity and femininity?[18] If femininity equates to vulnerability, and vulnerability is an inevitable aspect of the human condition at different times of life, being feminine might actually promote resilience because it means accepting the reality of vulnerability and not avoiding it. Women might be stronger because they can get their heads around being vulnerable and are comfortable with using social relationships to get through those times. Whereas men, ironically, might be made more vulnerable if the gender-role stereotype and expectation for them encourage them to socially isolate and hide their need for care from others.[19]

My last question is about that minority (estimated at about 30 per cent) of people who have never experienced any childhood adversity. They are clearly a fortunate group, but we do not know much about them, and it could be useful to find out more about them and what makes them so fortunate. Is it in fact good fortune, and how long does it last? And there are other questions about this 'lucky' group. Could lack of experience of trauma make people vulnerable later because they lack understanding of how to survive pain and fear? Might that lack of understanding be a liability in some circumstances? For example, if the people who are making policy decisions about access to and funding of health and social care are people who have never been ill or suffered vulnerability, they may struggle to understand how important good care is to recovery. That lucky 30 per cent of people who have not experienced trauma may also not understand how lucky they are, and might see that luck as 'normality', finding it harder to imagine what it is like to be vulnerable or unwell or frightened and easier to dismiss vulnerability as 'poor choices'. So, I am thinking that at the level of policy-making, we might need new assumptions about what is 'normal' for societies, if having an adversity-free childhood is far from being the norm.

We will need good-quality answers to these questions if we are going to take human development across the lifespan seriously, because the evidence suggests that childhood adversity has major public health implications which we will all pay for. This goes beyond the issue of violence prevention and reduction, although given its costs and its consequences, preventing violence by preventing its childhood origins would seem to be an obvious priority. But for now we will need to use what we are learning about trauma as a risk factor for violence as part of any strategy for rehabilitating offenders and helping them change their minds for the better. That is the theme of my next lecture.

4: Can we change violent minds?

Can people who have been violent to others really change their minds for the better? In thinking about this question, I was reminded of a case history about a fifty-five-year-old woman – let's call her Mrs Jenkins. Mrs Jenkins told her family that she was no longer interested in doing housework. This change of behaviour and attitude caused her family concern because in the past, Mrs Jenkins had held traditional views about her roles as mother and wife and had been hugely house-proud. Therefore, to her family, her explanation that she had just had enough of housework was not reassuring. They thought there might be something seriously wrong with her, plus this new behaviour was causing a problem for her husband in terms of who was going to do the housework instead.

The GP took the family's concern seriously and referred Mrs Jenkins to a neurologist, who sent her off for a brain scan. This revealed that she had a huge meningioma (a benign brain tumour) in her frontal cortex. The presence of this tumour was thought to explain Mrs Jenkins' aberrant thoughts about not doing housework, and neurosurgery successfully removed the meningioma. It is not recorded what her husband felt when Mrs Jenkins recovered from her brain surgery and continued to insist that she was no longer interested in carrying out housework.

We can learn two things from this story: first, that if women change their minds about housework, not even brain surgery will change it back. But more seriously, we also learn that humans can and do change their minds about issues that are important to them. Mrs Jenkins' change of mind may have been relatively trivial, but in this lecture I want to explore whether and how violence perpetrators can change their minds for good. I am going to discuss some research on this subject, and why we (the public) might also need to change our minds about offender rehabilitation.

The problem of changing violent minds is one that is important to all of us, if only financially. The UK spent approximately £6 billion on the prison estate for the financial year ending in April 2023, and this expenditure may well rise in future years.[1] The costs of incarcerating people as a form of risk management are getting bigger, as judges impose longer sentences, and the average cost of detention in prison is now £51,724 per prisoner per year.[2] But economic evaluations suggest that increasing prison terms is not good value for money; even if there is a deterrent effect, it is modest at best and the value is outweighed by the huge costs of incarceration.[3]

The research on what helps violence perpetrators change their minds for the better is important to me personally because the hospital where I work plays one small part in the much bigger national and international efforts to reduce violent recidivism. As a therapist (and someone who has sought therapy), I know that most people who come to therapy are seeking a change of mind which they hope will change their lives and, crucially, the ways in which they relate to others. In that sense, I am like those violence perpetrators in hoping that over time, therapy will help us change our minds for good. My experience is that most violence perpetrators who come for therapy are hoping that they can let go of their old ways of thinking and lead a new life as part of a relational community.

Sadly, little media attention is paid to the provision of interventions for offenders, nor the outcomes, which are generally positive, especially for violence perpetrators. This lack of attention causes a risky information bias because it leads to unwarranted pessimism about people's potential for change, and presents an oversimplified view about an issue that is important to us as citizens and taxpayers.

Interventions in prison

So what do we know about studies of prison interventions for violence perpetrators? Some recent reviews find some grounds for optimism about the efficacy of such programmes. It seems that offering *any kind* of therapeutic intervention to offenders has a positive effect on reducing the risk of recidivism; a paper by Theresa Gannon and colleagues suggested that recidivism was halved for those who had treatment compared to those who did not. A study by Laceé Pappas and Amy Dent from 2023 suggests that the effect is especially strong for young offenders who are convicted of serious violence.[4] Skills training and restorative justice interventions are more effective than interventions that involve surveillance, control, deterrence and discipline. In fact, programmes that emphasise punishment and control may actually *increase* the risk of reoffending on release.[5]

One major review by colleagues in Oxford was more cautious about the benefits of therapeutic interventions in prison, pointing out that many studies are too small to make good-quality inferences.[6] They also pointed out that such interventions may well be ineffective if they are not integrated with social interventions that are known to reduce the risk of recidivism, such as accommodation, education, employment and financial security. But even this most cautious of studies found that one particular kind of intervention was associated with recidivism reduction, namely prison therapeutic communities (PTCs).

These programmes have been around for over half a century and are available in prisons in many countries, including Norway, the Netherlands, Spain, Sweden and England. They offer violent offenders a chance to look at their lives, past and present, examine with people like them how they came to lead a violent life, and explore what they need to do to stay safe in future and to make amends where they can. Some focus mainly on recovery from addiction and substance misuse, but most also look at personal relationships and ways to improve agency and a sense of social responsibility. Not only do they seem to be effective in terms of risk reduction, they are described as one of the few cost-effective mental health interventions for offenders.[7]

I want to emphasise that participating in a PTC or any kind of violence-reduction programme is not an easy option. In fact, *avoiding* such programmes is the easy option because participation involves a close look at what has gone wrong in the past and an examination of the distorted thoughts, emotions and beliefs that made violence seem reasonable. People who engage in these programmes often experience shame, fear, remorse and grief, and that's painful. When I gave my third Reith Lecture at Grendon, one of the prisoners said that attending the therapeutic programme was incredibly hard, adding, 'You see the truth of yourself in other people, and the truth hurts.'

Changing your mind means being ready to be uncertain about what you believe and know, and to take a chance on having a new thought, which may also be painful. Successful therapy of any kind means taking responsibility for what goes on in your mind and understanding that you are the author of the stories you tell yourself. I am thinking now of Luke, a man who killed when he was high on drugs (he was probably mentally ill at the time as well). He found participating in group therapy for people who had killed excruciating to start with, saying, 'I felt so exposed.' He ran away after the first session and told me he wouldn't consider going back, but a year or so later he found the courage to rejoin. Over the four years I have known him, I have seen his mind change in the way he relates to others, from the silent, paranoid man who glowered at anyone who passed him to becoming a warm man who supports others and who values the trust he feels able to place in others. Articulating how bitterly he regrets his offence has expanded his awareness of his human connections to others: his victim and the family of his victim, as well as his own family, from whom he was estranged.

Rehabilitation works better than shaming

Of course, some people will argue that violence perpetrators deserve to be isolated, belittled and shamed because of what they have done, and these people will be sceptical about the value of rehabilitation programmes. I urge those who feel that way to look at the work of Homeboy Industries (HBI), which is the largest gang-rehabilitation programme in the world.[8] Working in southern Los Angeles since 1988, it offers hope to thousands of men and women coming out of prison, having served time for violence. The Homeboy vision is that radical acceptance and compassion are the most effective ways to help people rediscover their capacity for goodness and reduce their risk of violence. This attitude of kinship, not exclusion, is scaffolded by a variety of social enterprises, including employment opportunities, help with housing and education, and, especially, help with mental health and addiction.

The success of the Homeboy approach is consistent with what has already been shown: that the risk of people reoffending decreases when they feel socially connected and valued, and when offered a chance to contribute like other people. This is because despair and hopelessness *increase* the risk of violence, rather than decreasing it; the founder of HBI reckons that all the young people he sees who join gangs do so *because* they are suicidal.

This is why the World Health Organization has emphasised preventing childhood trauma and improving young people's mental health as a way of decreasing the later risk of engaging in violent offending.[9] Conversely, denigrating and shaming offenders is not only ineffective psychologically, it may increase violence risk in future by setting the emotions of anger and despair like concrete in the minds of prisoners. These bad outcomes are especially obvious in young men incarcerated at an early age, and some US research suggests that increasing the 'dose' of incarceration decreases the chance of positive outcomes.[10]

The value of restorative justice

It may be argued that it is natural for victims of violence to feel vengeful and that making perpetrators feel horrible in prison is a kind of justice for them. I understand those feelings and they are not alien to me in any way. But what is striking is that they are not universal or inevitable. Over the last three decades, a different kind of justice has been tried: restorative justice (RJ), which brings victims and perpetrators together, and which has been shown to be beneficial for both parties and to reduce recidivism. RJ interventions are in use across the world.[11] They can be used at any point in an offender's engagement with the criminal justice system, from arrest to imprisonment and all points in between. Both victims and perpetrators describe feeling that RJ is helpful, and a 2013 review of RJ programmes found that reoffending was indeed reduced in those who complete RJ compared to those who do not.[12]

Restorative justice is a deep and delicate process, much harder than just turning away in fear or hatred. It involves people in a dialogue of dignity and tragedy where they speak honestly about their anger, their rage and their pain. The value to the victim is a chance to face the person who hurt them and convey in their own words what they suffered and the cost of the perpetrators' actions to them. The value to the perpetrator is that they must own responsibility for what they did, and they also get a chance to articulate their sense of remorse and regret. Although neither party is required to give either an apology or forgiveness, the UK Restorative Justice Council found that 90 per cent of victims get an apology from the perpetrator, compared to 19 per cent who go through the usual criminal justice process.

I have seen first-hand how complex and painful an RJ process can be. I remember Kenny, who was another member of one of our homicide groups, and who had also killed his mother when he was mentally unwell. Like many people who have committed family homicide like this, he became highly suicidal in the initial stages of his recovery process, but he made good use of the homicide group by exploring his feelings of guilt, shame and deep, deep remorse. He also brought to the group the anxiety he felt when his father wrote to him, expressing a wish to meet. This meeting took months to prepare for, and I think everyone was anxious about how it would go. And from what we heard, the meeting was very hard for both Kenny and his father; their speech together was halting and the pain between them was palpable. It could hardly be otherwise. But Kenny was able to tell his father that he was sorry, and how he knew that that alone could not make up for his father's loss. And Kenny could listen to his father's story, and especially his confusion about both loving and hating his son in equal measure. It was not a Hollywood ideal of tears, embraces and forgiveness but, rather, the beginning of a conversation which I imagine is still ongoing.

I could give you more data about the cost-effectiveness of restorative justice: of how it saves £9 for every £1 spent in the criminal justice process, or could save £7,000 per offender if implemented in the youth justice system.[13] Victims of violence describe feeling empowered by it, and at least one study has found that they suffer reduced rates of PTSD.

Could we change our minds about offender rehabilitation?

So PTCs and restorative justice can help individual offenders change their minds for good. I want now to think about the change of mind *we* might need to make as a society: what we might need to think about as communities of citizens who contribute a lot of money to offender management and have a big stake in making it work.[14]

Let's start big, with national happiness. Each year there is an international analysis of which countries of the world are happiest. In 2024, Finland won the number-one spot, but Denmark, Iceland, Sweden and Norway were all in the top ten. Out of interest, I checked the imprisonment rates for these countries, and found that they were all well below the European average, let alone the international one. I wonder if there's a link between national happiness and increased emphasis on rehabilitation of offenders? Intriguingly, these countries also have lower recidivism rates, despite not sending people to prison so much. If you're wondering, the UK was at number twenty, so not bad. But I wonder if we could do better by considering whether we too might be prepared to fund more parental support and affordable childcare, and restore the child and adolescent mental health services that have been decimated in the last ten years in the UK.

Another change we could make is to enhance the training of our prison officers. A recent review of what makes prison programmes really effective in reducing recidivism found that having trained prison staff run the programmes worked better than using only specialist psychological professionals.[15] His Majesty's Prison and Probation Service states clearly that offender rehabilitation is part of its mission, but at present only a fraction of our prison officers get any training in mental health, or on how imprisonment might affect people who have experienced lots of childhood trauma, or even the best ways of managing prisoner anger and distress. Given that at least a third of prisoners are struggling with a range of mental disorders, *not* training the prison staff who interact with prisoners every day must put those staff at a disadvantage, and may increase their anxiety.[16] Two recent studies of women prisoners and prison officers in a women's prison examined both groups' knowledge and experience of women's trauma prior to imprisonment. Several participants (staff and prisoners) reported that a minority of prison officers seem not to understand the importance of past trauma in the lives of prisoners, which can lead to conflicts and disputes that the prisoners experience as abusive. Better training for prison officers might prevent this happening with especially vulnerable inmates.[17]

Compare the UK's situation with that of Norway, whose correctional department also states that offender rehabilitation is a priority. To become a correctional officer (not a guard) in a Norwegian prison, you must complete two years of academic study, then do a training year in a prison, after which you can go on to complete a university degree in correctional studies. The starting pay is actually *lower* than in the UK, but the rate of dropout is also lower because Norwegian prison officers see the value of staying in their roles to build relationships with prisoners and develop greater skills in the rehabilitation of offenders. Helping prisoners succeed on release is seen as vocational in terms of supporting people to become better citizens, and also making an investment in ensuring that their society is safer for everyone.

In Norway, offenders are punished by losing their liberty. This is the only punishment. Imprisonment does not lead to the loss of ordinary human and citizen rights, and inflicting further suffering on prisoners is seen as ethically and legally unjustifiable. Contrast this attitude with the one we have in the UK, where prisoners are not seen as citizens, and where making them suffer in prison is seen as 'justice'.[18] The pain and suffering of imprisonment include constant fear, overcrowding, lack of time in association with others and lack of health care provision. Prisoners also suffer the sense of public shame and belittling (typically articulated in the newspapers and now on the internet), which describes them as 'depraved' or 'evil' or 'monsters'. This pain is exacerbated by the howls of public outrage if and when any prisoner receives ordinary, decent treatment, like access to books or therapy, as if provision of care to prisoners is a zero-sum game.

We all understand that revenge is a powerful human emotion, but there is little evidence that it facilitates justice; we only have to look at the current wars across the world to see how inflicting revenge on those who hurt us leads to more violence, not less. So we have to ask ourselves whether our wish to hurt people who have hurt us is affordable, or whether we could spend our money better. It costs £101,938 per year to keep some non-violent prisoners in prison; wouldn't some of that money be better spent on getting them housing and treatment for their mental health problems, which in turn might reduce their risk of reoffending?[19]

Treating prisoners badly may superficially feel like solace to a grieving, rageful survivor or the family of a victim, but the evidence suggests that it doesn't work. In fact, the wish to hurt a prisoner mirrors the mind of the violence *perpetrator*. If you are wishing harm to someone right now because they hurt you, you know what it is to be an offender. That hatred, rage and wish to hurt lead to further suffering and hopelessness, and the loss of happiness. I know this because I see it in the men and women I work with, whose violence in a waste of rage leads to loss of all that makes life happy. I also know that we urgently need more research to identify those people who can't be rehabilitated and will never be safe enough to release, because they will be our biggest cost. And because human hearts and minds are unpredictable, sometimes people we think have changed their minds for good may reoffend.

But that kind of catastrophe is rare. The cost–benefit analysis makes it clear that we can no longer afford to create huge populations of people whose experience in prison shames, denigrates and belittles them, and spend billions locking them up because we fear them.[20] Instead, we could try having faith in the published evidence that violence perpetrators can change for good. Perhaps we also need to have a bit more faith in ourselves that we could let our vengefulness go, and find other ways to transform our grief and pain. For me, this is why it is vital that we offer much more long-term care and support for victims of violence; living with feelings of grievance, resentment, murderous rage and vengefulness is grim, and it can poison people's lives and minds in unexpected and dreadful ways.

I want to end by telling you about Jacob Dunne, who killed a young man with a single punch when he was nineteen. Mr Dunne wrote a book about his experience of being a violence perpetrator and a prisoner, and it is a remarkably honest account of how he came to kill and what happened afterwards.[21] He is very clear that his experience in prison did not change his mind for good at all; in fact, when he left, he still justified what he had done and still saw violence as a way of maintaining his 'honour' as a young man. It was only afterwards, when he met his victim's parents through the RJ process and listened and talked with them in depth about the killing and its impact, that he was able to re-evaluate who he was and the kind of person he wanted to be in the future. He now works with the very same groups of young men that he used to be part of, to try and help them find better ways to manage those emotions of loss, isolation and despair that make violence more likely.

There is so much more that could be said. But we really do know what we need to do to change violent minds. We know that we need to identify vulnerable young people early and support them with better ways of managing anger and despair so that they do not turn to addiction, nor the industry that supports it. If they are imprisoned, we need to ensure that all violence perpetrators get access to programmes that have been shown to be effective, and we need to think about sentencing in terms of risk management, rather than revenge. The evidence tells us that a range of interventions can make a difference in terms of risk reduction and recidivism – the investment is worth it. I passionately believe that if we spent less on building bigger and bigger places to treat people badly, we might have more money to support all those who, as victims of violence, whether as children or adults, suffer and rage and grieve.

One last question to ask ourselves: what would I want for my son or daughter if they did a terrible thing? What would I want for myself? I would suggest that most of us would want a chance to make good, if we could; to be shown mercy even if we don't deserve it. We ask offenders what kind of people they want to be in the future; we could ask ourselves the same question.

Afterword
Is there a link between human goodness and mental health?

I have been blessed to work in a profession which I find endlessly fascinating, and I enjoy teaching and lecturing on different aspects of the work. But it is a sad truth that my lectures are always on terrible and tragic topics; I never get to give talks about roses or Bach or George Clooney or anything nice. Especially, I rarely get to explore more positive aspects of the human experience, such as compassion, hope and goodness.

So, in this extra essay, I want to discuss human goodness and pose a question that I often ask myself, which is about the relationship (if any) between goodness and mental health. So much of forensic psychiatry involves meeting people who have done terrible things, acts outlandish in their cruelty. These are often actions that make others say, 'You'd have to be mad to do something like that,' implying, I suppose, that if a person were mentally healthy, they would never do anything dreadful or unlawful.

I am thinking now of Martin, who killed his father in an out-of-the-blue attack, and then mutilated the body by breaking open the chest and removing the heart. He did all this in front of a terrified man who had just come to read the water meter. And when the police came to arrest Martin (and interview the poor man from the water board), they clearly assumed that he was mentally ill because his actions made no logical sense; this killing was a paradigm example of senseless, meaningless violence which seems to imply a loss of rationality. Martin was indeed found to be mentally ill at the time of the killing and was a patient in secure psychiatric hospitals for many years. During that time, he also spent many hours in therapy, but I think it's fair to say that we never really completely understood the significance of his actions, and neither did he. He accepted that his attack on his father, which he bitterly regretted, was entirely caused by his mental illness, and he consented to take medication and be supervised for the rest of his life.

So we could say that Martin was a good man when he was mentally well, and those of us who work with patients like Martin therefore assume that being mentally well will help keep people from doing bad things. But a moment's thought about this presents a counter-argument, which is that surely there are people who do horrible things when they are mentally well? This question was naturally explored at length at the Nuremberg trials, where most of the Nazi high command and senior officers had psychiatric evaluations as part of the proceedings. One or two were thought to have some clinically identifiable mental health problems; for example, Julius Streicher, who published the anti-Semitic newspaper *Der Stürmer*, was described as paranoid. However, the majority were deemed to be mentally well. Indeed, most of them rejected any idea that they might have problems with their mental health because they saw themselves as having been the best and most honourable of soldiers in a good cause.

There have been similar attempts to 'diagnose' Hitler (and later Stalin also) with a variety of psychopathologies, as if the idea that people could consciously choose to do bad things is hard to accept. I explored an aspect of this idea in my second lecture, in which I discussed the concept of evil, arguing that anyone can get into an evil state of mind, but such a state rarely resembles the states of mind we see in patients in secure psychiatric hospitals. I find myself in agreement with those authors who have argued that evil is an absence of something good, and that, perhaps, evil states of mind arise when people fail to practise goodness.

What do we mean by goodness?

Like the word 'evil', goodness can elude easy definition. I wonder if this is because goodness (like evil) is not something which is 'out there', like an entity in the world, but, rather, is better understood as *a way of being* in the world, and especially a way of being in relationship *with something other than ourselves*. Unlike evil, goodness is something that is actively sought by many people at different times in their lives, not just in terms of doing good, but some sense of *being* good. There are layers of action here; some people might be content with being 'seen' as good, even while they secretly know that they are not. And we might also need to consider different senses of being good; for example, being 'good' in terms of 'function' or skill ('She is good at playing the piano') may be different to being good 'with people' in terms of relating to others. So 'good' can be used as an adjective to describe actions and states of mind, just as 'evil' is better used as an adjective, rather than a noun.

In an essay entitled 'Of Goodness and the Goodness of Nature', the philosopher Francis Bacon suggested that 'the inclination to goodness is imprinted deeply in the nature of man'.[1] This claim is supported by the striking similarities between accounts of goodness across different countries and cultures; for example, some version of the Golden Rule (i.e. treating others as you would like to be treated) exists in every part of the world in some form. Faith groups, humanists and atheists can all articulate the Golden Rule as a human duty, although they may use different kinds of argument to do so. The duty to treat others as you would like to be treated is also at the basis of most laws, especially in relation to criminal and civil offences in which one person has wronged and/or harmed another.

Historically, the study of how to be a good person was called the study of 'morality' or customs of a society, and it was the province of philosophers, and especially moral philosophers. The study of morality is the study of how we think about goodness, and its absence, and also of the claim that we exist in a universe where goodness has a fundamental meaning and rationality. Most of the world's oldest faiths are based on some account of human goodness and how to achieve it; for example, in Christian thought, goodness is the basis of who we are as humans, and departure from the practice of goodness tends to have bad consequences for society.[2] The late and much missed Frans de Waal had a different argument, based on his studies as a primatologist: he argued (like Darwin) that moral values are embodied in our primate heritage as group animals, and they reflect our need to be connected to one another in relationships that persist over time.[3] He had no doubt that goodness (especially in the sense of valuing others and helping them) could be seen in non-human primates like gorillas and chimpanzees.

What are the components of goodness?

Just as philosophers and theologians proposed the existence of seven deadly sins in human psychology, so classical authors such as Plato and Aristotle described nine virtues which were essential to goodness. Aristotle argued that by practising virtues, a person develops that character in which goodness not only exists but is preferred. Put another way, goodness becomes part of the personality and the general way that people relate to others.[4]

Aristotle's original nine virtues were wisdom, prudence, justice, fortitude, courage, liberality and temperance, and also included munificence and magnanimity, which were later dropped. The remaining seven were the so-called 'cardinal' virtues, 'cardinal' being derived from the Latin word meaning a 'hinge'. The cardinal virtues therefore act to connect and stabilise the mind so it can turn towards goodness, as a hinge stabilises a door that connects different spaces.

Similar lists of human virtues can be found in the Old Testament Book of Proverbs, the New Testament of the Christian Bible, especially St Paul's Epistles, in the writings of Buddha, the Chinese philosophers Confucius and Mencius, and in Hindu thought. We find echoes of the virtues in our laws and codes of practice like the Nolan Principles of civic life, and (arguably) in various international frameworks relating to human rights, such as the US Constitution and the European Convention on Human Rights.

I think it is intriguing that the virtues are not simply the opposites of the deadly sins, in the sense that they are not a list of negatives such as 'not being greedy' or 'not being slothful'. Instead, they offer a positive way of managing the ordinary stressors of human life. For example, the virtue of patience implies a capacity to maintain composure and to accept difficulties in life, whether they be with other people or in challenging situations. Temperance also implies a capacity for moderation in how we respond to life's troubles and demands, so that we manage distress without either acting it out or trying to avoid it by numbing ourselves with alcohol and drugs. Fortitude also implies a capacity for persistence and strength when things are hard. Wisdom and prudence suggest a careful approach to analysis of situations that are hard, learning from what others have learned about such situations, and taking time to reflect, rather than acting impulsively. It could be argued that liberality (or generosity) is an alternative to avarice and greed, and justice is about taking other people's claims to be seen and heard seriously. Justice and generosity are the most obviously relational of the cardinal virtues and arguably represent acknowledgement of the fact that we all live in communities and relationships which impact on our identity and how we live our lives.

Courage is a state of mind in which people face and manage their fear, which is one of our riskiest emotions in terms of social life. Prejudice, bigotry, anger and hatred all start with fear, and in a long and happy human life, each one of us will have to face and deal with its various forms. 'Courage' is derived from the Latin word for 'heart', and those who have courage do not necessarily feel brave or strong, but they somehow find the strength and 'heart' to do what they think is the right thing. It has been said that courage is the most beautiful of all the virtues because it makes all the other ones possible.[5]

I am thinking now of Steve Gallant, who, when he saw a man attacking people with a knife at a public event at the Fishmongers' Hall in London, joined with others to try and pin down the perpetrator, while trying to disarm him.[6] At that moment, he found the courage to do something risky to himself in order to help others, and his actions may have saved many lives. His actions are especially remarkable because at that time, Mr Gallant was out on day release, having served a long sentence for murder; in theory, getting caught up in *any* sort of fight could have lost him his liberty and got him sent back to prison. But he knew what the right thing to do was, even if it was risky for him, and he found the 'heart' to do it. He later received a civil gallantry award from the late Queen, and I was privileged that he attended my first Reith Lecture.

How can we be our best selves?

I commented earlier that goodness is a state of mind which reflects a way of being in the world, especially with other people. In this sense, a 'good' person embodies goodness in their sense of self and how they relate to other people, so that it is part of their personality and character. It's important to realise that our personalities are something we *do*, not something that we *have*; our personality is how we embody our personal sense of self in relationships with others. Our personalities grow and form during our childhoods; some aspects of our character can be identified early in our youth and persist across the lifespan, which makes it possible for us to say at school reunions, 'She's just the same now as she was then.' But there are aspects of our personalities that also change in response to environmental stressors like intense fear or grief, so that we can meet people we have known for a while and say, 'He's changed since he lost his wife.' Studies of exposure to trauma, especially in childhood, demonstrate how personalities can be changed by interpersonal experiences that involve high levels of emotional intensity.[7]

I am thinking now of Ted, a man in his fifties whom I saw when I was working in a trauma clinic. He had come at his wife's insistence because she said he had some personality change after a comparatively minor car accident. Ted had suffered an injury to his knee which had taken some time to heal; during this period he could not work, so he became bored, and he could not exercise, so he put on weight. His wife said that he was now hostile towards her in a way that she found disturbing; he had always been a man with 'a bit of an edge to him', she said, but this had been tempered by a good sense of humour and warmth towards people he cared for. Now she saw little warmth, and he seemed to relish bringing up conflicts relating to old family issues and belittling her interests.

When I saw him first, he was evidently irritable; he criticised his wife for raising the issue of trauma as an explanation for his mood, and was clearly annoyed at 'having to talk to a shrink' (in my experience, it is never a good sign when people use that word, because it is denigrating of the mind). But he did agree to come and see me again, and over time, it became clear that his accident had left him profoundly scared of becoming vulnerable and of losing his health and identity as a worker. He felt 'unmanned', and his losses (although temporary) made him angry, but the only person who was around to get angry with was his wife. As he acknowledged what was going on and how he felt, he was also able to say that he felt ashamed of being mean to his wife but, paradoxically, that sense of shame made him feel even more resentful towards her, as if she was to blame for shaming him.

What I found interesting about Ted's experience was how it was a milder, almost homeopathic version of what I often hear from people in prisons and secure hospitals. A person who had previously been mentally well and prosocial would gradually change to become mean and frightening to others, but their account of how they had changed would be an *externalised* story of how others had changed, and then they had changed in response. For example, Ted told me that he thought his wife was just being hypersensitive because she was going through the menopause, and that fact might be both true and relevant.

But what was missing from his initial account was any suggestion that *his* mind might have been changed in response to external events, i.e. that there had been an internal change in how he saw himself and his wife, which was relevant to understanding what was happening.

I could have diagnosed Ted with post-traumatic clinical depression and prescribed antidepressants, and we could have agreed that this depression had 'caused' him to be more irritable. Using that explanatory narrative, Ted wasn't 'mean', he was 'unwell', with a medical diagnosis. Treat the condition successfully, and Ted would become 'good' again as he became 'mentally well'. But I didn't think Ted's story was quite as simple as that, and although I did think he was depressed and I did suggest he try antidepressants, I thought that for Ted to 'recover' the man he used to be, he was going to have to think and reflect on how he felt about being 'unmanned'. He might also have to ask himself if he felt less 'unmanned' while he was making someone else feel small.

As with so many medical conditions, the pharmacological approach is definitely useful, but even the best and most effective medications probably work better when people are also offered an opportunity to think and reflect on what matters to them so they can make meaning of their experience.[8] Ted was brave; he took the medication *and* he took a chance on talking to me, and he gradually felt better in himself. He joined a group of other men of similar age at his gym who also had physical health issues, which helped him feel more 'normal', and he lost some weight. But I have to say that I thought that Ted's recovery was really complete when he told me how he had apologised to his wife for being mean and thanked her for supporting him when he was (as he said) 'in a bad place'.

Does therapy make you a better person?

Ted's story is also a reminder to me of a complex ethical question about any form of psychological therapy: namely, is therapy a morally neutral intervention? Or does it always fundamentally involve attention to human values and virtues? The reason this question arises is because, usually, when we go to see a doctor, we want them to make us better physically, regardless of whether we are good people with good intentions. A person who breaks his leg escaping from the police will still get the same treatment from his orthopaedic surgeons, regardless of whether he is planning to commit similar offences when recovered.

But psychiatric and psychotherapeutic treatments involve a change of mind, and that change of mind is anticipated ultimately to be prosocial. I doubt any therapist would agree to a request to help a person who sought to become crueller to other people (although I am sure most therapists would say, 'Let's talk about this'). In fact, it used to be argued that therapists like me were potentially acting *against* the interests of offenders by offering them therapy while they were incarcerated, because if imprisoned, they could not consent freely, and they might feel coerced into participation. (My long experience has taught me that this argument has no basis in reality, because the issue itself becomes a focus of therapeutic discussion, which changes the dynamic and helps people think about autonomy in different ways.[9])

But the process of changing minds for the better often involves people being open about parts of themselves or emotions that they fear or feel ashamed of and don't like to admit to. I'm thinking here of a young woman who gave a talk about her time in group therapy. She said that this had been incredibly helpful for her because, as she put it, 'I brought my ugly self to the group, and they accepted me . . . and then I could understand that part of me, and something changed.'

I found her insight and candour moving and illuminating, and it rang true for me, because I think that is exactly what happened for me when I was in therapy: I brought ugly and horrible parts of myself to the therapeutic space, and by naming them and looking at them compassionately, I was able to 'see' them in a different way. Often those 'ugly' parts of ourselves are an understandable response to past pain, but they have now outlived their usefulness *because* they belong to the past.

Most readers will know that there are myriad schools and techniques in therapy, some more evidence-based than others. But fundamentally, most successful therapies offer the same thing: a safe space to explore the uglier, meaner parts of our selves so we can change for the better. Some therapies help people think about those cognitive distortions I discussed in my second lecture, while others help people regulate painful emotions like anger and fear, which lead to conflicts, especially at those times when people feel uncertain and vulnerable. No therapy claims to make people more virtuous, but many do promote the prosocial virtues that seem to make people happier, like kindness, forgiveness and gratitude. And the practice of these non-classical virtues has the capacity to change our relationships with others for the better, so we can take a chance on having a new thought or perspective on who we are, who we have been and who we want to be.

One thing that therapies can do which can make people happier and more prosocial is help them relate to time in a different way. Anxiety and fear make people preoccupied with the future, whereas guilt and resentment keep them stuck in the past. Nearly all the most effective therapies help people focus on their present-moment experience, so that the past can be the past. And we all need to learn how to anticipate future experiences that cannot be known, let alone controlled. There is just not space in this essay to describe all the different therapies that try and help people feel better about themselves and their relationships.

But in the end, all the therapies are an invitation to reflect on what's really going on in your mind and to take it seriously, and the best, most effective ones also invite you to think about the reality of other people's minds and perspectives, even if they seem alien or disagreeable. We have to live with the reality of other people's minds, whether we like it or not: at work, in the street, and especially in those enduring relationships with friends, partners and family that seem to protect people from committing acts of violence. People who've experienced therapy as helpful don't just say that they 'feel better'; they usually say that they can now make better relationships at work and at home, perhaps because they feel more able to own and articulate their life story, and because they realise that they hadn't understood that most people feel the same.[10]

But what research into successful therapy also seems to suggest is that psychological health and well-being intersect with the virtues discussed above, especially patience, tolerance and self-control. A successful therapy can't change the past, but it can offer new ways of managing painful feelings from the past and provide hope for the future. We do this by paying more attention to what is happening right now with the people in our lives, and seeing that we have choices about how we react to others in the present, even if we didn't back then. Successful therapies also help us understand that other people have minds like our own; we may not always be able to 'read' or 'see' them accurately, but by imagining other minds, we might make deeper and richer connections to them. And having a network of connections is vital, because people who are socially isolated tend to have poorer physical and mental health, and they are over-represented among those who kill themselves and harm others.[11]

No man is an island: paying attention to our relational health

I want to conclude by suggesting that there may be a connection between good mental health, happiness and the traditional virtues and indicators of 'good' character. I am glad to say that the John Templeton Foundation in the USA is one academic body which is looking at this issue.[12] On its website there are accounts of research that looks at the connections between virtues like humility, gratitude and honesty and the ways that people form positive relationships with others. The foundation is investing $8 million to look at how 'good' character might be developed in the digital age, and it emphasises the importance of storytelling and imagination in this process, two things that are key to relational interventions in mental health.

We should also consider the Harvard Study of Adult Lives, which has followed a group of students for over eighty years to look at what life factors make for happiness and health. There are many publications from this study which find that the happiest people are also prosocial, with strong, enduring social relationships, and who give to their communities in different ways, including supporting the next generation by sharing wisdom and experience.[13] The one factor that makes a positive life less likely is alcohol addiction, which, as I have said elsewhere, is also a risk factor for general poor physical health and violence to others. The prosocial state of mind is life-enhancing and even life-extending for some, but the antisocial state of mind is associated with isolation, sadness and early death.

It is this research and others like it that makes me think that there is nothing 'normal' about cruelty and violence in humans. Humans are aware of their disposition for both goodness and cruelty; they tend to seek goodness and reject or avoid what Milton called their 'dark materials'.[14] Research into practising kindness and gratitude indicates that this can not only make us feel happier, but it also increases our sense of the prosocial and even makes us want to be better people.

So I wonder if we have a duty to stand up for goodness by practising virtues and taking other people's minds seriously – as seriously as our own. This includes paying attention to everyone; not just people like ourselves, but those who might seem different or even alien. A serious stance means being attentive to differences and similarities between people, and continuing to do so when this process leaves us feeling puzzled or uncomfortable. If goodness is a way of being with others in the world, then we might need to work on our capacity for courage to turn towards (and not avoid) those painful emotions of fear and anger, and by looking at them with compassion, perhaps help each other to let them go.

I will end with an old fable about a person who is offered a chance to see what Hell and Heaven are really like. They are first taken to Hell, where they see a big round table covered in delicious food. But each person seated round the table cannot access the food because they are only equipped with a spoon with an extremely long handle, which they cannot turn round towards their mouths because there is no space. Everyone at this table in Hell is screaming and raging with fear and hunger.

The visitor shudders and turns away to visit Heaven. To their shock and dismay, they are shown another similar table, with beautiful food on it, and people all around with the same long-handled spoons. But in this same situation, there is no raging or crying; rather, there is an atmosphere of joy and gratitude. The visitor bends down and whispers to one of the seated diners, 'How is it that you are all so happy here in Heaven, when you can't feed yourselves?' 'Ah, yes,' comes the response. 'We are often asked this. It is true that we cannot feed ourselves here, but we have learned that with our long-handled spoons, we can feed each other and be satisfied.'

Acknowledgements

It was a huge privilege and pleasure to give the 2024 Reith Lectures. I owe a huge debt of thanks to Mohit Bakaya for having the idea of violence as a theme in the first place and for asking me to give the lectures. I am also especially grateful to Jim Frank and Clare Fordham from the BBC Reith team, whose notes and comments on earlier drafts of the lectures were invaluable. As always, Eileen Horne and Sophie Lambert made me think of things I'd missed, and I am so glad and grateful that Laura Hassan made this Faber publication possible.

Endnotes

Author's note

1 *Global Study on Homicide 2013*, United Nations Office on Drugs and Crime, https://www.unodc.org/documents/gsh/pdfs/2014_GLOBAL_HOMICIDE_BOOK_web.pdf; *Global Study on Homicide 2023*, United Nations Office on Drugs and Crime, https://www.unodc.org/documents/data-and-analysis/gsh/2023/Global_study_on_homicide_2023_web.pdf

1: Is violence normal?

1 F. de Waal, 'The Chimpanzee's Sense of Social Regularity and Its Relation to the Human Sense of Justice', *American Behavioral Scientist*, 34 (3), 1991, pp. 335–49; F. de Waal, *Chimpanzee Politics: Power and Sex Among Apes* (JHU Press, 2007); R. Sapolsky, *A Primate's Memoir: A Neuroscientist's Unconventional Life Among the Baboons* (Simon and Schuster, 2007).

2 B. Masters, *Killing for Company: The Case of Dennis Nilsen* (Random House, 1985).

3 *Global Study on Homicide 2023*, United Nations Office on Drugs and Crime, https://www.unodc.org/documents/data-and-analysis/gsh/2023/Global_study_on_homicide_2023_web.pdf; *Homicide in England and Wales: Year Ending March 2023*, Office for National Statistics, https://www.ons.gov.uk/peoplepopulationandcommunity/crimeandjustice/articles/homicideinenglandandwales/yearendingmarch2023; *Homicide in Scotland 2023–24*, Scottish government, https://www.gov.scot/publications/homicide-scotland-2023-24/pages/main-findings; rate of violence falling: *The Nature of Violent Crime in England and Wales: Year Ending March*

2024, Office for National Statistics, https://www.ons.gov.uk/peoplepopulationandcommunity/crimeandjustice/articles/thenatureofviolentcrimeinenglandandwales/yearendingmarch2024

4 On 13 March 1996, a man killed sixteen children and a teacher in the primary school in Dunblane. Mr Maxwell lost a child in that massacre. F. Maxwell, 'Dunblane (1996)', in T. Maxwell (ed.), *When Trees Were Green: The* Scotsman *Articles of Fordyce Maxwell* (Martins the Printers, 2023), pp. 38–43.

5 M. Senior, S. Fazel and A. Tsiachristas, 'The Economic Impact of Violence Perpetration in Severe Mental Illness: A Retrospective, Prevalence-Based Analysis in England and Wales', *The Lancet Public Health*, 5 (2), 2020, pp. e99–106.

6 S. Zhong et al., 'Risk Factors for Suicide in Prisons: A Systematic Review and Meta-Analysis', *The Lancet Public Health*, 6 (3), 2021, pp. e164–74; S. Fazel, T. Ramesh and K. Hawton, 'Suicide in Prisons: An International Study of Prevalence and Contributory Factors', *The Lancet Psychiatry*, 4 (12), 2017, pp. 946–52. Although these studies do report that length of sentence and violence perpetration are risk factors for suicide, people detained for non-violent offences are at increased risk of suicide, especially if they have poor mental health. A study published in January 2025 found that those *released* from prison or serving sentences in the community are also at greatly increased risk of suicide.

7 Women's Aid, 'Women's Aid Launches "No More Years of Hurt" Campaign', 20 June 2024, https://www.womensaid.org.uk/womens-aid-launches-no-more-years-of-hurt-campaign-highlighting-the-spike-in-domestic-abuse-during-big-football-games; S. Kirby, B. Francis and R. O'Flaherty, 'Can the FIFA World Cup Football (Soccer) Tournament Be Associated with an Increase in Domestic Abuse?' *Journal of Research in Crime and Delinquency*, 51 (3), 2014, pp. 259–76, https://doi.org/10.1177/0022427813494843; A. Trendl, N. Stewart and T. Mullett, 'The Role of Alcohol in the Link Between National Football (Soccer) Tournaments and Domestic Abuse – Evidence from England', *Social Science and Medicine*, 268, 2021, 113457; R. Ivandić et al., 'Football, Alcohol, and Domestic

Abuse', *Journal of Public Economics*, 230, 2024, 105031.
8 P. Aylward, *Understanding Dunblane and Other Massacres* (Routledge, 2012); G. Adshead and E. Horne, *The Devil You Know: Encounters in Forensic Psychiatry* (Faber, 2021).
9 N. Wilkins, B. Tsao et al., *Connecting the Dots: An Overview of the Links Among Multiple Forms of Violence* (Atlanta, GA: National Center for Injury Prevention and Control, Centers for Disease Control and Prevention; Oakland, CA: Prevention Institute, 2014); N. Wilkins, L. Myers et al., 'Connecting the Dots', *Journal of Public Health Management and Practice*, 24, 2018, pp. S32–41.
10 S. Maruna and H. Copes, 'What Have We Learned from Five Decades of Neutralization Research?' *Crime and Justice*, 32, 2005, pp. 221–320.

2: Aren't they all evil?

1 W. Blake, 'A Divine Image', 1789.
2 S. Galderisi et al., 'Ethical Challenges in Contemporary Psychiatry: An Overview and an Appraisal of Possible Strategies and Research Needs', *World Psychiatry*, 23 (3), 2024, pp. 364–86; Graham Thornicroft, *Shunned: Discrimination Against People with Mental Illness* (Oxford University Press, 2006); J. Monahan, H. Steadman et al., *Rethinking Risk Assessment: The MacArthur Study of Mental Disorder and Violence* (Oxford University Press, 2021).
3 W. H. Auden, 'Herman Melville', in E. Mendelson (ed.), *Collected Poems* (Faber, 1994), p. 251.
4 C. R. Browning, *Ordinary Men: Reserve Police Battalion 101 and the Final Solution in Poland* (Penguin, 2001).
5 *Homicide in England and Wales: Year Ending March 2023*, Office for National Statistics, https://www.ons.gov.uk/peoplepopulationandcommunity/crimeandjustice/articles/homicideinenglandandwales/yearendingmarch2023; *Homicide in Scotland 2023–24*, Scottish government, https://www.gov.scot/publications/homicide-scotland-2023-24/pages/main-findings
6 ADE 651, https://en.wikipedia.org/wiki/ADE_651

7 H. M. Cleckley, *The Mask of Sanity: An Attempt to Clarify Some Issues About the So-Called Psychopathic Personality* (1941; C. V. Mosby, third edition, 1955; Dead Authors Society, 2023), although the Cleckley family have generously published it online: https://gwern.net/doc/psychology/personality/psychopathy/1941-cleckley-maskofsanity.pdf; R. D. Hare, 'A Research Scale for the Assessment of Psychopathy in Criminal Populations', *Personality and Individual Differences*, vol. 1, 1980, pp. 111–17; R. D. Hare, S. D. Hart and T. J. Harpur, 'Psychopathy and the *DSM-IV* Criteria for Antisocial Personality Disorder', *Journal of Abnormal Psychology*, 100 (3), 1991, p. 391.

8 B. X. Lee, B. E. Wexler and J. Gilligan, 'Political Correlates of Violent Death Rates in the US, 1900–2010: Longitudinal and Cross-Sectional Analyses', *Aggression and Violent Behavior*, 19 (6), 2014, pp. 721–8; T. L. Armstead, N. Wilkins and M. Nation, 'Structural and Social Determinants of Inequities in Violence Risk: A Review of Indicators', *Journal of Community Psychology*, 49 (4), May 2021, pp. 878–906, doi: 10.1002/jcop.22232. Epub 17 August 2019. PMID: 31421656; PMCID: PMC7278040.

3: Does trauma cause violence?

1 W. H. Auden, 'September 1, 1939', in E. Mendelson (ed.), *Selected Poems* (Faber, 1979), p. 86.
2 F. Bacon, 'Of Revenge', in *Essays or Counsels, Civil and Moral* (1625).
3 V. J. Felitti, R. F. Anda et al., 'Relationship of Childhood Abuse and Household Dysfunction to Many of the Leading Causes of Death in Adults: The Adverse Childhood Experiences (ACE) Study', *American Journal of Preventive Medicine*, vol. 14, issue 4, 1998, pp. 245–58; an earlier UK study that is not so well known: M. E. Wadsworth and D. J. Kuh, 'Childhood Influences on Adult Health: A Review of Recent Work from the British 1946 National Birth Cohort Study, the MRC National Survey of Health and Development', *Paediatric and Perinatal Epidemiology*, 11 (1), 1997, pp. 2–20; K. Hughes, M. A. Bellis et al., 'The Effect of Multiple

Adverse Childhood Experiences on Health: A Systematic Review and Meta-Analysis', *The Lancet Public Health*, 2 (8), 2017, pp. e356–66.

4 K. Hughes, M. A. Bellis et al., 'Adverse Childhood Experiences, Childhood Relationships and Associated Substance Use and Mental Health in Young Europeans', *European Journal of Public Health*, 29 (4), 2019, pp. 741–7; K. Hughes, K. Ford et al., 'Health and Financial Costs of Adverse Childhood Experiences in 28 European Countries: A Systematic Review and Meta-Analysis', *The Lancet Public Health*, 6 (11), 2021, pp. e848–57.

5 S. Wood, M. Bellis et al., 'Tackling Adverse Childhood Experiences: State of the Art and Options for Action', Public Health Wales NHS Trust, 2023, https://phwwhocc.co.uk/resources/tackling-adverse-childhood-experiences-aces-state-of-the-art-and-options-for-action

6 J. A. Reavis, J. Looman et al., 'Adverse Childhood Experiences and Adult Criminality: How Long Must We Live Before We Possess Our Own Lives?' *The Permanente Journal*, 17(2), 2013, p. 44; B. Hahn Fox, N. Perez et al., 'Trauma Changes Everything: Examining the Relationship Between Adverse Childhood Experiences and Serious, Violent and Chronic Juvenile Offenders', *Child Abuse & Neglect*, vol. 46, 2015, pp. 163–73, https://doi.org/10.1016/j.chiabu.2015.01.011; C. G. Malvaso, J. Cale et al., 'Associations Between Adverse Childhood Experiences and Trauma Among Young People Who Offend: A Systematic Literature Review', *Trauma, Violence, & Abuse*, 23 (5), 2022, pp. 1,677–94.

7 C. Heim and C. Nemeroff, 'The Impact of Early Adverse Experiences on Brain Systems Involved in the Pathophysiology of Anxiety and Affective Disorders', *Biological Psychiatry*, 46 (11), 1999, pp. 1,509–22; M. H. Teicher and J. A. Samson, 'Annual Research Review: Enduring Neurobiological Effects of Childhood Abuse and Neglect', *Journal of Child Psychology and Psychiatry*, 57 (3), 2016, pp. 241–66; E. M. Cooke, E. J. Connolly et al., 'A Systematic Review of the Biological Correlates and Consequences of Childhood Maltreatment and Adverse

Childhood Experiences', *Trauma, Violence, & Abuse*, 24 (1), 2023, pp. 156–73. But see Matthew Cobb for a cautionary view of what we know about brain architecture and the mind: M. Cobb, *The Idea of the Brain* (Profile Books, 2020).

8 See S. W. Porges, 'The Vagal Paradox: A Polyvagal Solution', *Comprehensive Psychoneuroendocrinology*, 16, 2023, 100200.

9 M. Szyf, 'DNA Methylation, Behavior and Early Life Adversity', *Journal of Genetics and Genomics*, 40 (7), 2013, pp. 331–8; M. J. Meaney, M. Szyf and J. R. Seckl, 'Epigenetic Mechanisms of Perinatal Programming of Hypothalamic–Pituitary–Adrenal Function and Health', *Trends in Molecular Medicine*, 13 (7), 2007, pp. 269–77; L. Cao-Lei, S. R. De Rooij et al., 'Prenatal Stress and Epigenetics', *Neuroscience & Biobehavioral Reviews*, 117, 2020, pp. 198–210; M. Szyf, 'Epigenetic Processes as Mediators of the Impact of the Social Environment', in *Epigenetics in Biological Communication* (Springer Nature Switzerland, 2024), pp. 131–76.

10 L. C. Aiello and R. I. Dunbar, 'Neocortex Size, Group Size, and the Evolution of Language', *Current Anthropology*, 34 (2), 1993, pp. 184–93; R. I. Dunbar, 'The Social Brain: Mind, Language, and Society in Evolutionary Perspective', *Annual Review of Anthropology*, 32 (1), 2003, pp. 163–81; R. I. Dunbar, 'The Social Brain: Psychological Underpinnings and Implications for the Structure of Organizations', *Current Directions in Psychological Science*, 23 (2), 2014, pp. 109–14.

11 H. F. Harlow, M. K. Harlow and S. J. Suomi, 'From Thought to Therapy: Lessons from a Primate Laboratory', in *Readings in Abnormal Psychology* (MSS Information Corporation, 1973), pp. 254–76.

12 A. N. Schore, 'Early Organization of the Nonlinear Right Brain and Development of a Predisposition to Psychiatric Disorders', *Development and Psychopathology*, 9 (4), 1997, pp. 595–631; A. N. Schore, 'Attachment and the Regulation of the Right Brain', *Attachment & Human Development*, 2 (1), 2000, pp. 23–47; D. Cicchetti, F. A. Rogosch et al., 'False Belief Understanding in Maltreated Children', *Development and Psychopathology*, 15 (4), 2003, pp. 1,067–91; D. Cicchetti, F. A. Rogosch, 'The

Role of Self-Organization in the Promotion of Resilience in Maltreated Children', *Development and Psychopathology*, 9 (4), 1997, pp. 797–815; M. Beeghly and D. Cicchetti, 'Child Maltreatment, Attachment, and the Self System: Emergence of an Internal State Lexicon in Toddlers at High Social Risk', *Development and Psychopathology*, 6 (1), 1994, pp. 5–30; A. Sylvestre, È. L. Bussières and C. Bouchard, 'Language Problems Among Abused and Neglected Children: A Meta-Analytic Review', *Child Maltreatment*, 21 (1), 2016, pp. 47–58.

13 A. Danese and C. S. Widom, 'Associations Between Objective and Subjective Experiences of Childhood Maltreatment and the Course of Emotional Disorders in Adulthood', *JAMA Psychiatry*, 80 (10), 2023, pp. 1009–16; A. Danese and C. S. Widom, 'Objective and Subjective Experiences of Childhood Maltreatment and Their Relationships with Cognitive Deficits: A Cohort Study in the USA', *The Lancet Psychiatry*, 11 (9), 2024, pp. 720–30.

14 K. Peltonen, N. Ellonen et al., 'Trauma and Violent Offending Among Adolescents: A Birth Cohort Study', *Journal of Epidemiology and Community Health*, 74, 2020, pp. 845–50; C. Burke et al., 'Adverse Childhood Experiences and Pathways to Violent Behaviour for Women and Men', *Journal of Interpersonal Violence*, February 2023, 38 (3–4), pp. 4,034–60. doi: 10.1177/08862605221113012

15 A. Testa et al., 'Adverse Childhood Experiences and Adult Household Firearm Ownership', *JAMA Network Open*, 2024, 7(8), e2428027. doi: 10.1001/jamanetworkopen.2024.28027 (reprinted).

16 C. S. Widom, 'Does Violence Beget Violence? A Critical Examination of the Literature', *Psychological Bulletin*, 106 (1), 1989, p. 3.

17 M. Salo, A. A. Appleton and M. Tracy, 'Childhood Adversity Trajectories and Violent Behaviors in Adolescence and Early Adulthood', *Journal of Interpersonal Violence*, 37 (15–16), 2022, NP13978–NP14007.

18 See Gilligan and Richards' discussion of toxic masculine stereotypes about selfhood and power, as found in Shakespeare's

plays, so it's not a new problem. J. Gilligan and D. A. Richards, *Holding a Mirror Up to Nature* (Cambridge University Press, 2021).

19 See Jonathan Haidt's interesting discussion about the effects of social media on boys and girls in J. Haidt, *The Anxious Generation* (Penguin Random House, 2024).

4: Can we change violent minds?

1 This report will give an idea of how that £6 billion figure is arrived at: *Increasing the Capacity of the Prison Estate to Meet Demand*, Ministry of Justice, HM Prison and Probation Service, National Audit Office, 4 December 2024, https://www.nao.org.uk/reports/increasing-the-capacity-of-the-prison-estate-to-meet-demand. In 2023–4, HM Prison and Probation Service (HMPPS) spent £3.56 billion on prisons, around 67 per cent of HMPPS's total net expenditure. But the service now estimates it will cost between £9.4 billion and £10.1 billion to deliver its portfolio, an increase of between £4.2 billion and £4.9 billion compared with its approved estimated funding of £5.2 billion, as at the 2021 spending review.

2 'Costs Per Place and Costs Per Prisoner by Individual Prison', Ministry of Justice, 21 March 2024, https://assets.publishing.service.gov.uk/media/65f4229810cd8e0011 36c655/costs-per-place-per-prisoner-2022-2023-summary.pdf

3 H. Wermink, J. Been et al., 'The Price of Retribution: Evidence from the Willingness to Pay for Short-Term Prison Sentences Compared to Community Service Orders', *Journal of Experimental Criminology*, 2023, pp. 1–32; E. K. Rose and Y. Shem-Tov, 'Does Incarceration Increase Crime?' July 2018, available at SSRN 3205613; O. Mitchell, J. C. Cochran et al., 'Examining Prison Effects on Recidivism: A Regression Discontinuity Approach', *Justice Quarterly*, 34 (4), 2017, pp. 571–96.

4 T. Gannon, M. Olver et al., 'Does Specialized Psychological Treatment for Offending Reduce Recidivism? A Meta-Analysis Examining Staff and Program Variables as Predictors of

Treatment Effectiveness', *Clinical Psychology Review*, 73, 2019, 101752; N. Papalia, B. Spivak et al., 'A Meta-Analytic Review of the Efficacy of Psychological Treatments for Violent Offenders in Correctional and Forensic Mental Health Settings', *Clinical Psychology: Science and Practice*, 26 (2), 2019, e12282; L. Pappas and A. Dent, 'The 40-Year Debate: A Meta-Review on What Works for Juvenile Offenders', *Journal of Experimental Criminology*, 19 (1), 2023, pp. 1–30.

5 D. L. MacKenzie and D. P. Farrington, 'Preventing Future Offending of Delinquents and Offenders: What Have We Learned from Experiments and Meta-Analyses?' *Journal of Experimental Criminology*, 11, 2015, pp. 565–95; D. M. Petrich et al., 'Custodial Sanctions and Reoffending: A Meta-Analytic Review', *Crime and Justice*, 50 (1), 2021, pp. 353–424.

6 G. Beaudry, R. Yu et al., 'Effectiveness of Psychological Interventions in Prison to Reduce Recidivism: A Systematic Review and Meta-Analysis of Randomised Controlled Trials', *The Lancet Psychiatry*, 8 (9), 2021, pp. 759–73.

7 M. Knapp and G. Wong, 'Economic Evaluations of Mental Health Interventions in Criminal Justice', *Criminal Behaviour and Mental Health*, 2023, doi: 10.1002/cbm.2286

8 Homeboy Industries: https://homeboyindustries.org

9 N. Wilkins, B. Tsao et al., *Connecting the Dots: An Overview of the Links Among Multiple Forms of Violence* (Atlanta, GA: National Center for Injury Prevention and Control, Centers for Disease Control and Prevention; Oakland, CA: Prevention Institute, 2014); N. Wilkins, L. Myers et al., 'Connecting the Dots', *Journal of Public Health Management and Practice*, 24, 2018, pp. S32–41.

10 E. S. Barnert et al., 'How Does Incarcerating Young People Affect Their Adult Health Outcomes?' *Pediatrics*, 139 (2), 2017, e20162624; L. A. Teplin et al., 'Prevalence, Comorbidity, and Continuity of Psychiatric Disorders in a 15-Year Longitudinal Study of Youths Involved in the Juvenile Justice System', *JAMA Pediatrics*, 175 (7), 2021, e205807; A. J. Harrison, J. A. Jakubowski et al., 'Patterns of Incarceration Among Youth After Detention: A 16-Year Longitudinal Study', *Children and Youth Services*

Review, 108, 2020, 104516. Professor Linda Teplin is a friend of mine; her latest study about the impact of a big 'dose' of incarceration on positive outcomes is due for publication in 2025.

11 *Handbook on Restorative Justice Programmes* (United Nations Office of Drugs and Crime, 2006).

12 L. W. Sherman et al., 'Are Restorative Justice Conferences Effective in Reducing Repeat Offending? Findings from a Campbell Systematic Review', *Journal of Quantitative Criminology*, 31, 2015, pp. 1–24, https://doi.org/10.1007/s10940-014-9222-9; J. Shapland, 'Evaluating Restorative Justice – According to Its Aims', European Forum of Restorative Justice, 29 November 2022, https://www.euforumrj.org/evaluating-restorative-justice-according-its-aims; College of Policing, 'Evidence Briefing', 18 January 2022, https://www.college.police.uk/guidance/restorative-justice/evidence-briefing

13 'Evidence Supporting the Use of Restorative Justice', Restorative Justice Council, https://restorativejustice.org.uk/resources/evidence-supporting-use-restorative-justice; A. M. Nascimento, J. Andrade and A. de Castro Rodrigues, 'The Psychological Impact of Restorative Justice Practices on Victims of Crimes – A Systematic Review', *Trauma, Violence, & Abuse*, 24 (3), 2023, pp. 1,929–47.

14 *World Happiness Report 2024*, https://worldhappiness.report/ed/2024

15 T. Gannon, M. Olver et al., 'Does Specialized Psychological Treatment for Offending Reduce Recidivism? A Meta-Analysis Examining Staff and Program Variables as Predictors of Treatment Effectiveness', *Clinical Psychology Review*, 73, 2019, 101752.

16 N. Rebbapragada, V. Furtado and G. W. Hawker-Bond, 'Prevalence of Mental Disorders in Prisons in the UK: A Systematic Review and Meta-Analysis', *British Journal of Psychiatry Open*, 7 (S1), 2021, pp. S283–4.

17 J. Kelman, R. Gribble et al., 'How Does a History of Trauma Affect the Experience of Imprisonment for Individuals in Women's Prisons: A Qualitative Exploration', *Women & Criminal Justice*, 34 (3), 2024, pp. 171–91; J. Kelman et al., 'Prison Officers' Perceptions of Delivering Trauma-Informed Care in Women's

Prisons', *Journal of Aggression, Maltreatment & Trauma*, 33 (10), 2024, pp. 1,258–79.
18 The 'pain of imprisonment' is an old term in criminology; see B. Crewe, 'Depth, Weight, Tightness: Revisiting the Pains of Imprisonment', *Punishment & Society*, 13 (5), 2011, pp. 509–29.
19 'Costs Per Prison Place and Costs Per Prisoner 2022 to 2023 Summary', UK government spending, transparency data, https://www.gov.uk/government/publications/prison-performance-data-2022-to-2023
20 K. Marsh and C. Fox, 'The Benefit and Cost of Prison in the UK: The Results of a Model of Lifetime Re-Offending', *Journal of Experimental Criminology*, 4 (4), 2008, pp. 403–23; D. S. Nagin, 'Deterrence: A Review of the Evidence by a Criminologist for Economists', *Annual Review of Economics*, 5 (1), 2013, pp. 83–105. There is also an excellent podcast called *Locked Up Living* (https://lockedupliving.substack.com/podcast) which may be of interest.
21 J. Dunne, *Right from Wrong: My Story of Guilt and Redemption* (HarperNorth, 2022).

Afterword: Is there a link between human goodness and mental health?

1 F. Bacon, 'Of Goodness and Goodness of Nature', in *Essays or Counsels, Civil and Moral* (1625).
2 D. L. Sayers, *The Mind of the Maker* (Methuen Continuum, 2004).
3 F. de Waal, 'Morality and the Social Instincts: Continuity with the Other Primates', *Tanner Lectures on Human Values*, 25, 2005, p. 1.
4 These ideas of virtue have been especially relevant for the helping professionals; for example, E. D. Pellegrino, 'Toward a Virtue-Based Normative Ethics for the Health Professions', *Kennedy Institute of Ethics Journal*, 5 (3), 1995, pp. 253–77, and J. Radden and J. Sadler, *The Virtuous Psychiatrist: Character Ethics in Psychiatric Practice* (Oxford University Press, 2010).
5 C. S. Lewis, *The Screwtape Letters* (Geoffrey Bles, Centenary Press, 1941; Collins paperback edition, 2012). See also Louisa Young's wonderful *The Book of the Heart* (Flamingo, 2004).

6 S. Gallant, *The Road to London Bridge* (Seven Dials, 2023).
7 This is a complex area with mixed results. See this review, which suggests that only a minority of people develop a personality change after trauma in adulthood: J. Munjiza, V. Law and M. J. Crawford, 'Lasting Personality Pathology Following Exposure to Catastrophic Trauma in Adults: Systematic Review', *Personality and Mental Health*, 8 (4), 2014, pp. 320–36. And the change may be positive: E. Jayawickreme, F. J. Infurna et al., 'Post-Traumatic Growth as Positive Personality Change: Challenges, Opportunities, and Recommendations', *Journal of Personality*, 89 (1), 2021, pp. 145–65. But the evidence relating exposure to repeated childhood trauma to later personality disturbance is stronger, presumably because trauma affects the emergence of a stable and organised personality, especially in adolescence; for example, J. G. Johnson et al., 'Childhood Maltreatment Increases Risk for Personality Disorders During Early Adulthood', *Archives of General Psychiatry*, 56 (7), 1999, pp. 600–6. This is an ongoing field of research and much depends on how trauma is 'measured'. Epigenesis is likely to be influential. See A. Danese, 'Annual Research Review: Rethinking Childhood Trauma – New Research Directions for Measurement, Study Design and Analytical Strategies', *Journal of Child Psychology and Psychiatry*, 61 (3), 2020, pp. 236–50.
8 J. M. Newby et al., 'Systematic Review and Meta-Analysis of Transdiagnostic Psychological Treatments for Anxiety and Depressive Disorders in Adulthood', *Clinical Psychology Review*, 40, 2015, pp. 91–110. And see this review of studies on how combining therapy with medication can be helpful: E. Karyotaki, Y. Smit et al., 'Combining Pharmacotherapy and Psychotherapy or Monotherapy for Major Depression? A Meta-Analysis on the Long-Term Effects', *Journal of Affective Disorders*, 194, 2016, pp. 144–52.
9 G. Adshead, 'Ethical Issues in the Psychotherapy of High-Risk Offenders', in M. Trachsel et al. (eds), *Oxford Handbook of Psychotherapy Ethics* (Oxford University Press, 2021).
10 J. M. Adler, L. M. Skalina and D. P. McAdams, 'The Narrative

Reconstruction of Psychotherapy and Psychological Health', *Psychotherapy Research*, 18 (6), 2008, pp. 719–34.

11 This is a huge domain of research. This recent review emphasises that the absence of actual relationships is key to risk, not just loneliness: J. Holt-Lunstad and A. Steptoe, 'Social Isolation: An Underappreciated Determinant of Physical Health', *Current Opinion in Psychology*, 43, 2022, pp. 232–7. See also this recent review about the possible effects on the brain of social isolation and discrimination: L. Brandt et al., 'The Effects of Social Isolation Stress and Discrimination on Mental Health', *Translational Psychiatry*, 12 (1), 2022, p. 398.

12 John Templeton Foundation: https://www.templeton.org/grant/mental-healthcare-virtue-and-human-flourishing-2

13 G. Vaillant, *Aging Well: Surprising Guideposts to a Happier Life from the Landmark Study of Adult Development* (Little Brown, 2003); G. Vaillant, 'Positive Aging', in S. Joseph (ed.), *Positive Psychology in Practice: Promoting Human Flourishing in Work, Health, Education, and Everyday Life* (John Wiley, 2015), pp. 595–612.

14 G. Adshead, 'Their Dark Materials: Narratives and Recovery in Forensic Practice', 2012, Royal College of Psychiatrists Publication Archives, https://www.rcpsych.ac.uk/docs/default-source/members/sigs/spirituality-spsig/spirituality-special-interest-group-publications-gwen-adshead-their-dark-materials-narratives-and-recovery-in-forensic-practice.pdf?sfvrsn=e0168f8c_2; S. Lyubomirsky and K. Layous, 'How Do Simple Positive Activities Increase Well-Being?' *Current Directions in Psychological Science*, 22 (1), 2013, pp. 57–62.

Also by Dr Gwen Adshead and Eileen Horne

Coming in February 2026

Unspeakable

Survival and Transformation After Trauma

The Sunday Times *bestselling authors of* The Devil You Know *return with a life-affirming and myth-busting exploration of trauma, resilience and healing.*

A widow dares not utter her husband's name. A prisoner of war buries the memories of his ordeal. A child hostage is rendered mute. What happens when trauma goes unspoken?

The pioneering psychiatrist and psychotherapist Dr Adshead invites us to witness her work with patients struggling in the wake of a range of distressing and painful life events. What is the quality of their survival? Who and how do they want to be now? With her help, these courageous people step out of the darkness of shame and fear to discover new possibilities, and find that sometimes the hardest words to say out loud are the very ones to set us free.

Suffused with hope, *Unspeakable* powerfully shifts our understanding of the meaning and outcomes of trauma.

faber